A Gift for

_____

Presented by

_____

I Wish
I Knew
That

I Wish I Knew That

Cool Stuff You Need to Know

Steve Martin

Mike Goldsmith, Ph.D.

Marianne Taylor

Reader's Digest

The Reader's Digest Association, Inc.
New York, NY / Montreal

A READER'S DIGEST BOOK

Copyright © 2011 Buster Books

All rights reserved. Unauthorized reproduction, in any manner, is prohibited.

Reader's Digest is a registered trademark of The Reader's Digest Association, Inc.

First published in Great Britain in 2010 by Buster Books, an imprint of Michael O'Mara Books Limited,
9 Lion Yard, Tremadoc Road, London SW4 7NQ

FOR MICHAEL O'MARA BOOKS
Editor: Elizabeth Scoggins
Illustrator: Andrew Pinder
Designer: Zoe Quayle

FOR READER'S DIGEST
U.S. Project Editor: Barbara Booth
Project Production Coordinator: Nick Anderson
Senior Art Director: George McKeon
Executive Editor, Trade Publishing: Dolores York
Associate Publisher, Trade Publishing: Rosanne McManus
President and Publisher, Trade Publishing: Harold Clarke

Library of Congress Cataloging-in-Publication Data
Martin, Steve, 1962 Oct. 18-
  I wish i knew that : cool stuff you need to know / Steve Martin, Mike Goldsmith, and Marianne Taylor.
    p. cm.
  Includes index.
  ISBN 978-1-60652-340-7
  1. Handbooks, vade-mecums, etc.--Juvenile literature. 2. Science--Juvenile literature. 3. Math--Juvenile
literature. 4. Geography--Juvenile literature. 5. Literature--Juvenile literature. 6. History--Juvenile
literature. 7. Arts--Juvenile literature. 8. Civilization, Classical--Juvenile literature. I. Goldsmith, Mike, Dr.
II. Taylor, Marianne, 1972- III. Title.
  AG106.M385 2011
  031.02--dc22

                              2011014889

Reader's Digest is committed to both the quality of our products and the service we provide to our
customers. We value your comments, so please feel free to contact us:
     The Reader's Digest Association, Inc.
     Adult Trade Publishing
     44 S. Broadway
     White Plains, NY 10601

For more Reader's Digest products and information, visit our website:
www.rd.com (in the United States)
www.readersdigest.ca (in Canada)

Printed in the United States of America

3 5 7 9 10 8 6 4 2

CONTENTS

Introduction: Getting
ahead of the Class   9

Sounds Like ...   44
Let's Figure This Out   45
Languages of the World   47

LITERATURE STUFF   11

Shakespeare, in Short   12
Poets Corner   18
Classic Reads   22

CLASSIC STUFF   51

A Dip into the Classics   52
Ancient Languages   55
The Seven Wonders   57
Mythologically Speaking   59

MUSIC AND ART STUFF   29

A Brief History of Music   30
The World of Art   32

HISTORY STUFF   65

All the U.S. Presidents   66
Classified   70
How Cold Is a Cold War?   71
British Kings and Queens   72

LANGUAGE STUFF   35

In Search of Conquest   73
The Parts of Speech   36
Exploring the Globe   74
Putting a Sentence Together   40
Troubled Times   75
Unusual Terms   42
In Times of War   76

Some Algebra Magic 110
What Are the Chances? 112
Mathematical Greats 114

GEOGRAPHY STUFF 79

Countries, Continents, and
    Capital Cities 80
The United States 85
Tallest, Largest, Longest 86
How Land Is Shaped and
    Changed 88
The Water Cycle 90
Weather and Climate 91
Human Impact 93
Geological Time, in Brief 94

MATH STUFF 97

What's in a Number? 98
A Number of Questions 101
Compare and Contrast 102
Weird Numbers 104
Measuring, to Be Precise 106
Jump into Geometry 108

SCIENCE STUFF 117

First Physics 118
The Laws of Motion 119
Electricity and Magnetism 121
Space, Time, and All That 122
Gravity and Black Holes 123
Quick Chemistry 124
The Periodic Table 127
Chemical Compounds 130
Beginners Biology 132
Getting under Your Skin 133
Microlife 135
Where Did You Come From? 136

Index 138

INTRODUCTION:
GETTING AHEAD OF THE CLASS

Have you ever shocked your classmates by knowing something they didn't? Cool, isn't it?

In this book, you will discover lots of exciting things your teachers haven't mentioned—and revisit some of the things they have.

Find out the names of all the countries in the world and their capital cities. Discover how a black hole works and if a cold war really is cold. Read about an enormous island of floating plastic in the Pacific Ocean.

There are lots of bite-size chunks of information, from history and geography to math and science. There are even several sections on literature and language to make sure you get things right when you write.

Rather than a whole pile of books, you can get a taste of all these different subjects with just this one. In no time at all, you'll be able to impress your friends and family with a hundred interesting tidbits. Better still, you'll stay on top of the curve and way ahead of your classmates!

LITERATURE STUFF

SHAKESPEARE, IN SHORT

William Shakespeare, or the Bard (meaning poet), wrote some of the world's best-known plays and poems. He wrote funny plays known as comedies, along with sad plays, called tragedies, and several known as "problem plays," which are very entertaining but neither comedies nor tragedies. Here are some brief introductions to his most famous plays to help you bluff your way through until you can see them at the theater yourself.

Hamlet

Hamlet, the Prince of Denmark, is a troubled young man. His father, the king, has been murdered, and his mother has married his father's brother, Claudius, after only a few weeks.

One night the ghost of the king appears to Hamlet and reveals that Claudius murdered him. He asks Hamlet to seek revenge, but Hamlet wants to find more proof of the murder first. To do this, he pretends to be driven crazy by grief and puts on a play for Claudius that tells the story of a murder similar to that of the king's. It makes it very clear that the king has been murdered by his brother. When Claudius reacts nervously to the play, Hamlet is convinced he is guilty.

Hamlet goes to confront his mother in her room, but he thinks he can hear Claudius hiding behind a curtain and tries to stab him. Unfortunately, rather than Claudius, he has murdered Polonius, the father of Ophelia, a girl Hamlet once loved. The news shatters Ophelia, and she drowns herself.

These terrible events lead to more revenge, and this time Polonius's son, Laertes (pronounced LA-yer-tees), decides to punish Hamlet. Claudius sets up a duel between Hamlet and Laertes, but he gives Laertes a poisoned sword to make sure that Hamlet dies. Laertes fatally stabs Hamlet, but during the fight the two men accidentally switch weapons, and Hamlet also wounds Laertes with the poisoned sword.

A wounded Hamlet then manages to stab Claudius, but at that moment, his mother drinks from the poisoned wine that Hamlet had prepared for Claudius. Laertes, Hamlet, his mother, and Claudius all die—not really a happy ending.

Romeo and Juliet

This is the story of a young couple from two rival families, the Montagues and the Capulets. Romeo and Juliet fall in love instantly when they meet at Juliet's family party and are later secretly married by Friar Laurence. However, Tybalt, a cousin of Juliet's, is angry that Romeo came to the party uninvited and challenges him to fight. When Romeo refuses, his friend Mercutio fights instead and is killed. Romeo murders Tybalt in revenge and is sent away as punishment, leaving Juliet behind.

This wouldn't be so bad, except that Juliet's family, who still have no idea that she is married, arrange a wedding between Juliet and her cousin, Count Paris. To avoid Juliet's getting stuck with a second husband she doesn't want, Friar Laurence comes up with a plan.

The plan involves Juliet drinking a potion to make her appear dead. The idea is that Romeo will come back and rescue her from her tomb. Sadly, for both Romeo and Juliet the plan goes disastrously wrong when a message, reassuring Romeo that Juliet is only sleeping in the tomb, gets lost. Poor Romeo returns home believing his wife is dead. Stricken with grief, he kills himself, and when Juliet wakes up, she kills herself, too.

The Montagues and Capulets finally decide to stop being enemies, but it's all too late for Romeo and Juliet.

Now that's what you call a tragedy.

Macbeth

People often call this the "Scottish play" rather than saying the name "Macbeth" out loud. This is because, traditionally, the play is said to be unlucky. Superstitious actors hope to avoid accidents by not mentioning the M word.

When the play begins, Macbeth and his friend Banquo, both generals for King Duncan of Scotland, meet three witches— the "weird sisters." They tell Macbeth that he will be made thane (a nobleman) of Cawdor and later become king. However, they also tell his friend Banquo that his sons will be kings, not Macbeth's. When Macbeth becomes a thane, he and his scheming wife, Lady Macbeth, decide to kill King Duncan to hurry the witches' predictions along. But even when Macbeth is king, he is not satisfied, because he knows that Banquo's sons, rather than his own, will someday inherit the throne. So he has Banquo killed,. Banquo's ghost then drives Lady Macbeth crazy, and she dies.

The weird sisters give Macbeth another prophecy—that he will be safe until Birnham Wood comes to Dunsinane (Macbeth's castle). This seems so impossible that Macbeth believes his position as king is secure. A short time later, however, King Duncan's son, Malcolm, brings his army, camouflaged with branches from Birnham Wood, and Macbeth is killed, fulfilling the witches' prophecy.

Othello

This play shows how jealousy can make a mess of a great romance. Othello, a brave general, falls in love with and secretly marries Desdemona, the daughter of a senator. However, an enemy is soon plotting against him.

When Othello promotes a young soldier named Cassio to lieutenant over Iago, a more experienced soldier, Iago is furious. He gets revenge by convincing Othello that Desdemona is having a relationship with Cassio. Iago makes sure that Othello overhears Cassio discussing his love for a woman, and Othello assumes that it must be his wife, Desdemona. Othello's anger gets worse when Desdemona's handkerchief (planted by Iago) is found in Cassio's room.

Othello is so jealous that he ends up killing Desdemona, even though she has done nothing wrong. When Iago's trickery is revealed, Othello is devastated and kills himself.

So if you fall in love, remember the play's warning: Jealousy is a "green-eyed monster."

Much Ado about Nothing

On the way home from battle, Prince Don Pedro and his men, Claudio and Benedick, are invited to stay in Messina by Leonato, the governor of the city. There, Claudio is reunited with Leonato's daughter, Hero, whom he once loved.

Unfortunately, Claudio and Hero are driven crazy by the constant arguing between Beatrice (Leonato's niece) and Benedick. They decide to trick Beatrice into believing Benedick loves her and to convince Benedick that Beatrice loves him. Meanwhile, Don Pedro's evil brother, Don John, tricks Claudio into thinking Hero loves someone else. Claudio is so angry that he even abandons Hero on their wedding day.

Eventually, Claudio discovers the truth about Hero, and as Benedick and Beatrice have indeed fallen in love, the four of them decide on a double wedding.

The Tempest

A powerful wizard named Prospero and his daughter, Miranda, have been stuck on a magical island for 12 years after Prospero's brother, Antonio, cast them adrift at sea. On the island are two servants—a spirit named Ariel, and Caliban, the half-human son of a witch.

During their time there, Antonio, with the help of Alonso, the King of Naples, steals his brother's title of Duke of Milan. When Alonso and Antonio and several crew members sail past the magical island on the way back from Alonso's daughter's wedding in Africa, Prospero conjures up a violent storm—a tempest—to try to destroy the two men.

When the survivors of the shipwreck struggle to shore, Ariel helps Prospero take his revenge, tormenting Antonio and Alonso. In the meantime, Alonso's son, Ferdinand, has met and fallen in love with Miranda.

Eventually, Prospero, Antonio, and Alonso manage to mend their differences. Prospero gets his title back, and they all leave the island together. A favorable wind (a final gift from Ariel) speeds them home, where Miranda and Ferdinand marry, uniting the kingdoms of Milan and Naples.

POETS CORNER

Poetry is everywhere—in songs, advertising slogans, movies, and television. Here is a selection of some of the most well-known poets in history, with the names of the poems that made them famous. You may even enjoy reading some of them!

Samuel Taylor Coleridge

(Born 1772, died 1834)

Coleridge wrote only two famous poems, but what successes they were. "Kubla Khan," and the mysterious and scary "The Rime of the Ancient Mariner," which tells the story of a sailor who kills a large bird called an albatross and then suffers terribly for his crime.

Emily Dickinson

(Born 1830, died 1886)

Dickinson's poems deal mostly with loneliness and death—after all, her home overlooked a cemetery! They contain only a few short lines, and many lack any title at all, yet they speak volumes and have made her one of the most prominent poets in America. Surprisingly, only about a dozen of her 1,800 poems were published during her lifetime. It wasn't until four years after her death that her younger sister discovered Dickinson's poems and submitted them for publication so that her literary prowess could be shared with the rest of the world.

T. S. Eliot

(Born 1888, died 1965)

As well as his poems for adults such as "The Wasteland," Eliot wrote a book of poems for children, called *Old Possum's Book of Practical Cats,* which was the inspiration for a famous musical called *Cats.*

Ralph Waldo Emerson

(Born 1803, died 1882)

Born in 1803 in Boston, Emerson was the son of a Unitarian minister, who died when Ralph was only eight years old. He was very close to his mother and siblings and was raised in a very strict household. At just 14 he enrolled at Harvard and later married and settled in Concord, Massachusetts. Emerson is known for his strong belief in independent thinking and felt that not all learning comes from books. He loved to entertain, and his guests included many free thinkers, poets, and authors, such as Nathaniel Hawthorne, Louisa May Alcott, and Henry David Thoreau. He also loved to travel to Europe, where he became friendly with Samuel Taylor Coleridge and William Wordsworth. Some of Emerson's most famous poems are "Celestial Love," "Eros," and "Concord Hymn."

Robert Frost

(Born 1874, died 1963)

Probably second only to Walt Whitman (page 21) as the "great American poet," Frost won the Pulitzer Prize three times. His works include "Stopping by Woods on a Snowy Evening" (no doubt you'll hear the famous line *And miles to go before I sleep* sometime in the near future) and "The Road Not Taken" (*Two roads diverged in a wood, and I—/I took the one less traveled by*).

Rudyard Kipling

(Born 1865, died 1936)

Author of *The Jungle Book* and *Just So Stories,* Kipling was also a brilliant poet. His poem "If" was chosen as Britain's favorite poem in 1995.

Edward Lear

(Born 1812, died 1888)

As well as his famous poem "The Owl and The Pussy Cat," Lear created bizarre characters for his poems, such as the Pobble (who had no toes), the Quangle-Wangle (with a marvellous hat), and the Dong (with a luminous nose).

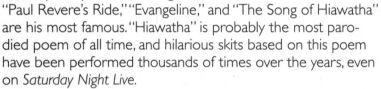

Henry Wadsworth Longfellow

(Born 1807, died 1882)

He is known for his lyric poetry— those with rhyming schemes that express personal feelings. "Paul Revere's Ride," "Evangeline," and "The Song of Hiawatha" are his most famous. "Hiawatha" is probably the most parodied poem of all time, and hilarious skits based on this poem have been performed thousands of times over the years, even on *Saturday Night Live*.

Edgar Allan Poe

(Born 1809, died 1849)

His very name conjures up images of dark and creepy tales of murder, revenge, torture, and insanity, and people in his day did not take well to his stories because they were just too scary. Nevertheless, Poe's poem *The Raven* became an instant success, and many of today's books and movies borrow ideas from Poe's works.

William Shakespeare

(Born 1564, died 1616)

Best known for his plays, Shakespeare was also a great poet, writing more than 100 sonnets (14-line poems), including the famous love poem that begins, "Shall I compare thee to a Summer's day?" (See also "Shakespeare, in Short," page 12.)

Walt Whitman

(Born 1819, died 1892)

An American poet, Whitman spent much of his life working on his poetry collection, *Leaves of Grass*. He kept releasing new versions of the book until he died. Whitman struggled to support himself through most of his life. He lived on a clerk's salary and modest royalties from his poems, and he spent most of his money to buy supplies for patients he nursed during the Civil War.

William Wordsworth

(Born 1770, died 1850)

This major English Romantic poet helped to launch the Romantic Age in English literature with *Lyrical Ballads,* a joint collection of poems with his close friend Samuel Taylor Coleridge. However, many consider Wordsworth's masterpiece to be **The Prelude,** a semiautobiographical poem of his early years that was first titled "To Coleridge." Later Wordsworth became Britain's Poet Laureate—a poet appointed a member of the royal household by the British monarch who is expected to write poems celebrating great national or royal events—and he remained so until his death.

CLASSIC READS

In any bookstore or library, you'll discover tales of magic and fantasy, pirates and shipwrecks, of things that happened long ago and of adventures from far away. The only trouble you may have is deciding which book to read first. Here is a quick guide to some of the most exciting reads from children's literature that you should be able to find easily.

If you read and enjoy these books, you may want to pick up some of the titles suggested below each one.

The Wonderful Wizard of Oz

(L. Frank Baum)

When people think of *The Wizard of Oz*, they most likely think of the movie, but the novel that came first is worth reading, too. You'll discover lots of things that aren't in the film at all. Something that may surprise you is that L. Frank Baum wrote 15 books about Oz, so there are many more to enjoy. In this first book, just as in the film, Dorothy is whisked away from her home in Kansas by a tornado. She lands in a strange land called Oz, where she travels with the Tin Man, the Cowardly Lion, and the Scarecrow. Only if she can reach the Emerald City and find the Wizard of Oz will Dorothy be able to get home.

You may also like: *The Lion, the Witch and the Wardrobe* and *The Chronicles of Narnia* by C. S. Lewis

Call of the Wild

(Jack London)

A dog named Buck is taken from a comfortable life on a farm and sent to the frozen north to haul a dog sled. Buck adapts quickly and is soon leader of the sled team. However, when the dogs are sold to a group of inexperienced men searching for gold, things do not go well.

A man named John Thornton rescues Buck, and they form a strong friendship, although Buck finds the "call of the wild" (his natural instincts) hard to resist.

You may also like: *White Fang* also by Jack London

The Secret Garden

(Frances Hodgson Burnett)

The story opens in India and is centered around little Mary Lennox, a sickly, spoiled girl born to rich British parents who are extremely self-absorbed and busy with extravagant parties. They neglect Mary and want nothing to do with her. Her parents suddenly die of cholera, so she is sent to England to live with her uncle, who is still mourning the loss of his wife who died 10 years earlier. To escape his sad memories, he constantly travels abroad, leaving Mary to be cared for by his housekeeper. The only person who has any time for the little girl is the chambermaid, Martha Sowerby, who tells Mary about a locked, walled garden that was the late Mrs. Craven's favorite place. With the help of a robin, Mary finds the key to the secret garden buried outside and discovers that in it all things seem possible.

You may also like: *A Little Princess* by Frances Hodgson Burnett and *Jane Eyre* by Charlotte Bronte

The Adventures of Tom Sawyer

(Mark Twain)

In a village in the American South, next to the Mississippi River, Tom and his friends are always misbehaving. When they become pirates and sail away to an island in the middle of the river, their families think they've drowned. The boys sneak home and reappear at their own funeral! However, things become much more serious when Tom and his friend, Huckleberry Finn, witness a murder.

You may also like: *Huckleberry Finn* by Mark Twain and *Robinson Crusoe* by Daniel Defoe

Anne of Green Gables

(L. M. Montgomery)

A grown-up brother and sister named Matthew and Marilla Cuthbert request a boy from the orphanage to help on their farm, called Green Gables. When a girl named Anne arrives instead, they let her stay. Matthew and Marilla grow to love Anne, but her vivid imagination soon gets her into trouble. Anne competes with a boy named Gilbert Blythe to be top of the class at school, which leads to some of the best tantrums ever written.

You may also like: *Pollyanna* by Eleanor H. Porter, *Heidi* by Johanna Spyri, and the *Little House* series by Laura Ingalls Wilder

The Wind in the Willows

(Kenneth Grahame)

When Mole visits a river for the first time, he makes friends with Ratty, Toad, and Badger. In the first of many adventures, Toad is arrested and sent to prison for stealing a motor car. He manages to escape in disguise, but when he returns home, he finds that his house, Toad Hall, has been taken over by a group of ferrets and weasels. He and his friends gather together to recapture Toad Hall.

After reading this, you'll never think of your local riverbank the same way again!

You may also like: *Tarka the Otter* by Henry Williamson and *The Hobbit* by J. R. R. Tolkien

The Jungle Book

(Rudyard Kipling)

This collection of stories includes "Mowgli's Brothers," which became the classic animated film *The Jungle Book*. This particular story tells of a young boy brought up in the jungle with characters such as Shere Khan, a tiger determined to kill him, Bagheera, a wise panther, Baloo, a lazy old bear, and Kaa, a cunning python.

Other stories include *Rikki-tikki-tavi,* an action-packed tale about a mongoose who saves a family from cobras, and *Toomai of the Elephants,* about a young boy who witnesses the magical sight of a legendary elephant dance.

You may also like: *Watership Down* by Richard Adams

Old Yeller

(Fred Gipson)

Set in the rough wilderness of early frontier Texas, this is a timeless coming-of-age tale of a boy named Travis and his big yellow dog. When Travis's father leaves for several months on a cattle drive, Travis is left to care for the farm all by himself and has to cope with many hardships with the help of his dog Old Yeller.

You may also like: *My Friend Flicka* by Mary O'Hara, *Black Beauty* by Anna Sewell, and *National Velvet* by Enid Bagnold

Treasure Island

(Robert Louis Stevenson)

In one of the most famous swashbuckling tales ever, young Jim Hawkins finds a treasure map and sets sail on the Hispaniola to find the treasure. While at sea, Jim discovers that the ship's cook, Long John Silver, and many of the crew are pirates. When they reach the island, the double-crossing and violence begins.

You may also like: *Twenty Thousand Leagues Under the Sea* by Jules Verne

Little Women

(Louisa May Alcott)

The author based this story on her own family life. It tells the story of four sisters—Meg, Jo, Beth, and Amy March. Set at the time of the American Civil War, the girls' father is away working as a chaplain for the army. The March sisters are poor, but they make the best of what they have. The story follows them as they grow and have many adventures and romances.

You may also like: *Emma* by Jane Austen

MUSIC
AND ART STUFF

A BRIEF HISTORY OF MUSIC

The history of classical music in Europe and the Americas can be divided into several periods, each with different styles and often with well-known stars. Jump right in with this brief guide to some of the most important periods.

Medieval

Most music that is still known from this period is religious—in particular, Gregorian chants, which are named after the 6th-century Pope, Gregory. These were written in "plainsong," which means that everyone sings the same tune together.

Renaissance

During the Middle Ages, a lot of the knowledge that had been gained from the Greeks and Romans was lost. The Renaissance (which means rebirth) began in Italy in the 14th century and was a time of rediscovery. People began to think about science, art, and culture again, and music became a more important part of entertainment as well as of religion. Even King Henry VIII of England wrote music. Between marrying, divorcing, and beheading wives, Henry wrote his own catchy folksongs (but he didn't compose *Greensleeves*, as many people say).

Baroque

By the Baroque period (roughly 1600 to 1750), instrument makers had developed sophisticated musical instruments. This meant that composers, such as Handel, Vivaldi, and Bach, could write even more interesting music. Vivaldi, who wrote hundreds of pieces, is familiar to many people because of his violin concerto, *The Four Seasons*, which conveys the feeling of each of the seasons in a year.

Classical

The Classical period went from the mid-18th century to around 1820. Top composers of the age included Mozart, Haydn, Schubert, and Beethoven. Beethoven gradually lost his hearing. He was completely deaf for the last few years of his life, but he continued to write music. When his *Ninth Symphony* was performed for the first time in 1824, Beethoven had no idea how much people were applauding until a musician made him turn to look at the audience.

Romantic

Beethoven's third symphony, *Eroica*, which he completed in 1804, was the first Romantic symphony. By the time he died in 1827, the Romantic period was fully under way and lasted into the 20th century. Composers such as Strauss, Verdi, and Puccini were able to make money from their music because it was so popular. Skilled solo musicians, including a man named Paganini, also became superstars of the day. People even described him as a "devil" because he could play such incredibly difficult music.

20th Century

Among many great 20th-century composers, such as Prokofiev, Shostakovich, Gershwin, and Copland, is Igor Stravinsky, a Russian composer, who wrote the music for many popular ballets. One of these— *The Rite of Spring*—caused a riot at its first performance in Paris.

THE WORLD OF ART

In the history of art, there have been many different "movements" (when groups of artists work in similar styles). Here are some of the most well known to start you off so that the next time you're walking around an art gallery, you can impress everyone with your superior knowledge.

Renaissance

In the same way that the Renaissance was important to the world of music (see page 30), it also gave much more freedom to painters and sculptors. Renewed interest in the ancient world made the subjects of science, literature, and art very popular. Leonardo da Vinci, who excelled in them all, is one of the most famous people of the Renaissance.

YOU KNOW WHAT? I'VE GONE OFF IT.

Florence, in Italy, was the center of Renaissance art for two centuries. A powerful family called the Medici, who lived there, were patrons to artists, including Michelangelo. He is known for his painting on the ceiling of the Sistine Chapel in the Vatican.

Baroque and Rococo

In the 17th century, artists such as Caravaggio developed the Baroque style—a grand and dramatic way of painting that influenced the designs of buildings at the time, too.

Baroque lasted until the 18th century, when it developed into the Rococo period—a more delicate and decorative style used by artists such as Canaletto.

Romanticism

In the 1800s many artists—Constable, Turner, and Blake, for example—developed a more romantic style. This meant that their paintings were more colorful and wild than those before, which had been painted following strict rules.

Arts and Crafts

In the 1850s Victorians were used to very over-the-top decoration and ornaments in their homes. The development of factories meant that these objects could be made in large numbers. However, artists such as William Morris preferred objects to be simple, well-made, and handcrafted.

Impressionism

In 19th-century France, a group of artists that included Monet and Degas developed new ideas about painting. They used color in a different way to capture an "impression" of objects and scenes, rather than painting them to look like photographs. For example, instead of painting a blue flower using only blue paint, they added areas of dark purple in the shadows or pale orange where light reflected on the edge of a petal.

Expressionism

In the late 19th and early 20th century, Expressionist artists such as Edvard Munch often exaggerated the shapes and colors of the things they painted to show how they felt at the time, or how they felt about a particular subject. Munch, for example, painted a famous picture called *The Scream,* which is full of bright, swirling colors and shows a person with his mouth wide open in horror and his hands clasped to the sides of his head.

LANGUAGE STUFF

THE PARTS OF SPEECH

The names of the different jobs that words do are called the parts of speech. There are nine of them:

Nouns

Nouns are naming words. Some nouns name particular people or places (your friend John or the planet Earth, for example) and are called proper nouns. They start with a capital letter.

Anything that is a kind of person (boy, parent), a kind of place (city, countryside) or a kind of thing (book, television) is called a common noun. Some nouns describe a group of people or things, such as a team or a pack. These are called collective nouns. Not all nouns name objects that you can see. Words such as Tuesday and happiness are also nouns.

Verbs

Verbs are often called "action words." They tell you what a person or thing is doing or being: run, give, cook, be, and talk are all verbs. When a verb is written out with the word *to* before it—*to run, to cook, to be*—it is called the *infinitive*.

Adjectives

An adjective describes a noun and gives you extra information about it. For instance, you could just say, **The woman bought a car.** But if you say, **The** *rich* **woman bought a** *fast* **car,** you know more about her and her car because of the adjectives *rich* and *fast.*

Adverbs

Adverbs describe verbs and give you more information about what is going on. The sentence, **The rich woman drives the car,** will do, but, **The rich woman drives the car** *carefully,* gives more detail.

Many adverbs answer the questions how, when, where, or why, and many of them end in "-ly." *Carefully, quickly, quietly,* and *loudly* are all adverbs.

You can also use adverbs to describe adjectives. In the sentence, **The** *incredibly* **rich woman drives carefully,** the word *incredibly* tells you how rich the woman is.

Adverbs can even be used to describe other adverbs, as in the sentence, **The incredibly rich woman drives** *somewhat* **carefully.**

Now we know that perhaps the woman doesn't drive as carefully as she should (and you will also have spotted that *somewhat* is one of those adverbs that doesn't end in "-ly").

Pronouns

A pronoun (*I, you, he, she, it, we, us, they,* and *them*) replaces a noun in a sentence, so that you don't have to keep repeating the noun. Rather than saying, **The woman drives the car every day and washes the car once a week,** try, **The woman drives the car every day and washes *it* once a week.** *It* replaces the word *car.*

The words *mine, yours, its, his, hers, ours,* and *theirs* are what are called possessive pronouns. They are used to show who owns something, as in the sentence, **I took the book because it was *mine.***

Conjunctions

You use conjunctions, or connecting words, all the time to join different parts of a sentence together (you'll learn about this on page 40). They join words, phrases, and clauses.

HEY! LISTEN TO ME.

The word *and* is the conjunction you use most often, but there are many more, including *or, but, nor, yet,* and *so.*

Prepositions

Prepositions are words that go before nouns in sentences. They show the relationship of one thing to another. Rather helpfully, a preposition tells you *where* something is—its position. There are quite a few, but the ones you'll see most are *by, to, in, into, for, from, of, between, with,* and *on.* So you could say, **The woman got *in* her car *with* her friends and went *to* the store.**

Interjections!

An interjection is a word that shows strong feelings, such as excitement or surprise. An interjection will often have an exclamation mark after it (especially if something is particularly exciting or surprising). Examples include *Wow! Ouch!* and *Hurray!*

Articles

There are two types of articles—definite and *indefinite. The* is the definite article. It tells you about a *particular* thing. *A* is the indefinite article—it could be any one of those things. For example, in the sentence **The boy loved *the* dog and his friend wanted *a* dog, too,** you can tell that the boy loved one particular dog, but his friend who would like a dog doesn't necessarily want *that* dog.

PUTTING A SENTENCE TOGETHER

You probably already know, of course, that a sentence begins with a capital letter and ends with a period (or a question mark or an exclamation mark). It's what goes between the capital letter and the period that can cause confusion. Writing in clear sentences is the best possible way to make sure that your writing makes sense to your readers (whether it's your teachers or the millions of people reading your first novel).

Subject

The subject is the person or thing that your sentence is about. The key is to remember that all sentences have a subject and a verb—they go hand in hand. The subject is whoever or whatever is *doing* the verb. For example, in the sentence, **Jack sang a song,** Jack is singing, so he is the subject.

Predicate

The predicate is the rest of the sentence—the part that isn't the subject: **Jack** *sang a song.* The predicate always includes the verb.

Object

The object is the person or thing that the verb is being done to. In the sentence above, the *song* is being sung by Jack, so the song is the object.

Clauses and Phrases

The sentence, **Jack sang a song,** is short and simple, but if you add groups of words, called clauses and phrases, you'll give your readers more detail.

A clause is a group of words that includes a subject and a verb. A phrase is a group of words that doesn't include a subject and verb and doesn't make sense on its own.

For example, in the sentence, **The boy sang a song while he grinned at his friends,** there are two clauses. The first, *The boy sang a song,* could be a sentence by itself. This is known as an *independent* clause. The second, *while he grinned at his friends,* could not be a sentence by itself. This is known as a *dependent* clause because it relies on the first clause to make a complete sentence.

However, in the sentence, **The young boy tried to sing a cheerful song,** the words, *The young boy* make up one phrase, with a noun in it (the subject of the sentence—our hero, Jack). This is what is called a noun phrase. The words *tried to sing* are another phrase (a verb phrase this time). Finally, the phrase *a cheerful song* is another noun phrase, and it is also the object of the sentence. None of these three phrases makes any sense on its own.

UNUSUAL TERMS

Nouns, verbs, clauses, and phrases are all terms you'll have to tackle at some point, but knowing these next seven will make quite an impact on your peers.

Allegory

An allegory is a story with a hidden meaning. For instance, *Animal Farm,* a book by George Orwell, sounds as though it might be a simple tale about farm animals. In fact, it's about the communist government in Russia during the 1930s. Orwell used the animals and their behavior to represent different kinds of people in the real world.

Cliché

Lots of sayings and expressions become dull if you hear them too often. When your teachers come out with an old saying such as, "You must have ants in your pants," when you are fidgeting, you can tell them they are using a cliché. (They might not appreciate it, though.)

Diphthong

A diphthong is when you pronounce one vowel sound and slide into another by changing the position of your tongue in your mouth. It's not as complicated as it sounds, though—when you say the word "boil," for example, the sound you are making is a diphthong. Try saying the following words aloud, too: "tail," "feel," "wear." Listen to how the vowel sounds join as you move from one to the next in the same breath.

Oxymoron

An oxymoron is not an insult. Oxymorons combine two expressions or words that contradict each other. If you deliberately forget to clean your room, for example, you may do so "accidentally on purpose," causing your mother to complain that it's a "fine mess" and to be so angry that there is a "deafening silence."

Paradox

A paradox is something that seems impossible yet may be true. If your parents make sure you do your homework, they may tell you they are "being cruel to be kind." It might appear impossible to be kind by being cruel, but they really mean that they're making you do something you'd rather not do so that you get a good education.

Rhetorical Question

A rhetorical question is one that you don't expect anyone to answer. For instance, if you say, "How should *I* know where your shoes are?" when a brother or sister has lost theirs, you wouldn't expect them to tell you exactly how they think you should know.

Tautology

Tautology means unnecessary repetition. For example, the expression "free gift" is a tautology because the whole point of a gift is that it's free, so it's better just to say "gift."

SOUNDS LIKE...

Homonyms

Some words have prefixes (at the beginning) and suffixes (at the end). In the word "homonym," *homo-* is the prefix, which comes from a Greek word meaning "the same." The suffix *-nym* comes from the Greek word for "name," so homonyms give the same name to different meanings. For example, the word "cross" has three homonyms: you can cross (travel over) a road, you can be cross (angry), and you can draw a cross (shape).

Homophones

The suffix *-phone* means "sound." Homophones are words that sound the same but are spelled differently. This sentence has three pairs of homophones: **The *band* was *banned* and so not *allowed* to play *aloud,* so you can't *hear* them *here.***

Synonyms

The prefix *syn-* also means "the same." Synonyms are words with the same, or nearly the same, meaning. For instance, if you want to write about a great vacation instead of using the word "great"repeatedly, why not mention the "lovely" weather or the "fabulous" beach?

Antonyms

The prefix *ant-* means "opposed to," so an antonym has the opposite meaning. An antonym of "good" is "bad" and an antonym of "wet" is "dry."

LET'S FIGURE THIS OUT

A figure of speech is a way of using words for effect. There are all sorts of figures of speech you can use to create different effects with language. Here are some of them:

Metaphor and Simile

Metaphors and similes are easy to confuse because they are both used to compare things. Similes describe one thing as similar to another thing, usually using the words "like" or "as." Your parents might say, "You're as good as gold," or, "You eat like a pig," for example. However, a metaphor says that a thing actually *is* something else. Your parents might say, "You're an angel," if you behave, or, "You're a little monster," if you don't, but you're not really an angel or a monster.

Alliteration

Alliteration is a group of words that begin with the same letter. For example, you could describe the "wild, windy weather" or "swirling, stormy sky." It is often used in poetry as a writing device to add emphasis.

Assonance

Repetition of vowel sounds in words is called assonance. It's also a technique that poets like to use to add dramatic effect, as in the first line of Edgar Allan Poe's poem *The Raven*:

> *Once upon a midnight dreary,*
> *while I pondered weak and weary.*

Here, the word "weak" uses almost the same vowel sound as the words "dreary" and "weary."

Hyperbole

If you say that you're starving, your parents don't call an ambulance, do they? What you really mean is that you are hungry, but you are exaggerating for effect. This is called hyperbole (which is pronounced hye-PER-boh-lee).

Onomatopoeia

This strange word (pronounced on-uh-mat-oh-PEE-ya) describes the use of words that sound like a sound. For instance, the "hiss" of a hissing snake sounds like the noise a snake makes. There are many words like this. For example, water "splashes," dropped pans "clatter" and bells "bong."

Personification

Personification gives an object or animal qualities that usually belong to people. If you write, "The sun smiled down on us," you are using personification because the sun doesn't really smile, people do.

LANGUAGES OF THE WORLD

There are thousands of languages in the world, but the best languages to learn depend upon where you live, where you might go on vacation, and what your interests are. Here are a few ideas, with some useful words to start you off.

Arabic

Arabic is the official language of more than 15 countries, including Morocco and Saudi Arabia. It is written in a different alphabet to English, so the translations here represent their pronunciation.

Hello—*Ahlan wa sahlan*
Good-bye—*Salam*
Please—*Min fadlak*
Thank you—*Shukran*

Spanish

As well as the official language in Spain and most of Central and South America, Spanish is also spoken by millions of people in the United States..

Hello—*Hola*
Good-bye—*Adiós*
Please—*Por favour*
Thank you—*Gracias*

German

German is spoken in Germany, Austria, and parts of Switzerland. It's from the same language family as English, so some words sound familiar, and many words mean the same in English and German—"hand," "name," and "warm," for instance—although they are pronounced slightly differently.

Hello—*Hallo*
Good-bye—*Auf Wiedersehen*
Please—*Bitte*
Thank you—*Danke*

French

French is an official language of more than 25 countries in the world including France, Belgium, Canada, Haiti and Mali.

Hello—*Bonjour*
Good-bye—*Au revoir*
Please—*S'il vous plaît*
Thank you—*Merci*

English uses many French words and expressions such as "rendezvous" (a meeting) and "en route" (on the way).

Japanese

Japanese is written in symbols rather than letters. There are three different sets of symbols, called *kanji, katakana,* and *hiragana.*

Hello—*Konnichiwa*
Good-bye—*Sayonara*
Please—*Onegaishimasu*
Thank you—*Arigato*

Japanese words such as *kimono* and *karate* are now used in everyday English.

Chinese

There are about 13 different varieties of the Chinese language, but the most widely used, by far, is Mandarin, which is the official language of the People's Republic of China. This is followed by Wu, Cantonese, and Min.

Hello—*Nǐ hao*
Good-bye—*Zàijiàn!*
Please—*Qí*
Thank you—*Xièxie*

CLASSIC STUFF

ON SECOND THOUGHT, MINOTAURS ARE VERY RARE. MAYBE I SHOULD LEAVE IT ALONE?

A DIP INTO THE CLASSICS

The subject of classics is the study of the history, art, and language of the ancient Greek and Roman civilizations.

Ancient Greece

The civilization of ancient Greece flourished between about 1,000 b.c. and 300 b.c. The Greeks had ideas about science, art, philosophy (thinking about the meaning of stuff), and politics that are still valued today. They came up with the idea of democracy—a political system in which ordinary people play a major role in governing themselves. It is the form of government that the majority of countries still use.

The Greeks were famous for their great philosophers. In the 5th century b.c., for example, a man named Socrates (SOK-ra-teez) asked his students questions, such as "What is right and wrong?" to help them think about the world around them. However, Socrates didn't leave anything written down, so Plato, one of his students, jotted it all down instead. Plato started The Academy in Athens, a forerunner to today's universities. His most famous student, Aristotle, became a great scientist as well as a philosopher.

Greece was also home to many talented storytellers. According to legend, a blind poet named Homer (not to be confused with Homer Simpson!) was said to have composed two very long poems, the *Iliad* and the *Odyssey*. People told each other his stories, and they were passed down from one generation to the next. However, writers such as Sophocles (SOF-o-kleez), Aeschylus (EE-ska-lus), and Euripides (you-RIP-id-eez) wrote lots of great plays, many of which are still performed today.

Life wasn't all studying for the ancient Greeks. They also held huge sporting events. One of these took place in a city called Olympia every four years. Men from all over the Greek world took part in events, such as javelin, discus, and chariot racing (women had their own competitions). Most sports were performed naked, as you can see here:

It was not until 1896 that the modern Olympic Games began (though people now prefer to get dressed first).

The Roman Empire

According to legend, Mars, the god of war, had two sons, Romulus and Remus, who were abandoned and cared for by a wolf. These brothers grew up to establish the great city of Rome in about 750 b.c. Although this story is highly unlikely,

Rome came to have immense power. Whenever the Romans conquered an area, their skilled craftsmen built towns with aqueducts (to bring water), bridges, bathhouses, theaters, and temples. They also built roads so that their army could move around quickly. You can still visit many Roman buildings in places all over Europe, North Africa, Asia, and the Middle East.

Despite their advanced civilization, the Romans could be very cruel. At the Colosseum, an arena in Rome, thousands of people watched as gladiators (warriors) fought to the death or as prisoners were thrown to lions.

For many years Rome was ruled as a democracy in a similar way to Greece. One of the men thought to have brought about the end of this democracy was Julius Caesar, a success-ful Roman general. He conquered many lands and, when he returned to Rome, made himself dictator for life. This meant that he was not elected by the people and had unlimited powers. It was short-lived, as he was assassinated soon after-ward, in 44 b.c., on the ides of March. (In the Roman calendar the 15th of March, May, July, and October and the 13th of every other month were all called the ides.)

For the rest of its history, Rome was ruled by emperors who had control of a highly disciplined army. The army was divided into sections called legions, which each had around 4,800 soldiers, plus supporting horsemen and archers.

Some of these emperors were not very pleasant. Nero, for example, who reigned from a.d. 54 to a.d. 68, was said to have murdered his own mother, executed his first wife, and may have murdered his second. His cruelty wasn't limited to his family; he was said to have had Christians burned to death at night to light up his garden. Eventually, the senate (the Roman government) had enough and sentenced Nero to death. Nero avoided execution by killing himself.

ANCIENT LANGUAGES

Many people describe ancient Greek and Latin, the language of ancient Rome, as "dead" languages. This is because no one has spoken them as everyday languages for a long time. However, they are still important today because thousands of words in modern languages come from Latin and Greek.

For example, in Latin the word for moon is *luna*—you'll spot it being used in English in words such as "lunar" (a lunar cycle is the cycle of the moon) and "lunacy" (another word for madness, because people once thought that the moon affected people's behavior). *Aqua*, the Latin for water, appears in "aquatic" (aquatic creatures live in water). *Ignis*, or fire, can be seen in words such as "ignite," which means to set alight.

In ancient Greek *angelus* meant "messenger," which is where the word "angel" comes from, because angels are described as messengers from God. The word for an octopus comes from *okto*, the Greek word meaning "eight." The link isn't always so obvious, though. For example, the word "hippopotamus" comes from the Greek *hippos* (horse) and *potamos* (river), so a *hippopotamus* is a "river horse."

Ancient words can be used in combination to make new words, too. For example, the words "tele" and "phone" mean "far away" and "voice," so a telephone is just a "far away voice."

The Greek Alphabet

Although the Romans wrote using pretty much the same letters as English, the Greek alphabet was (and still is) very different. You will probably come across some of these letters when you study math and science, but on the next page, you will find all of them listed in the correct order.

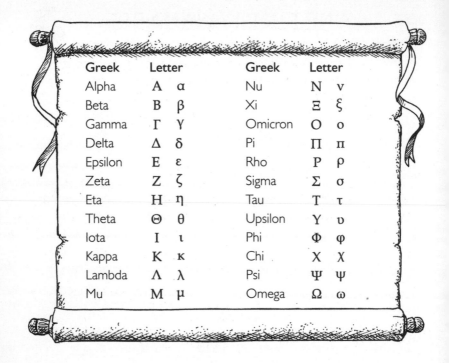

Greek	Letter		Greek	Letter	
Alpha	A	α	Nu	N	ν
Beta	B	β	Xi	Ξ	ξ
Gamma	Γ	γ	Omicron	O	o
Delta	Δ	δ	Pi	Π	π
Epsilon	E	ε	Rho	P	ρ
Zeta	Z	ζ	Sigma	Σ	σ
Eta	H	η	Tau	T	τ
Theta	Θ	θ	Upsilon	Y	υ
Iota	I	ι	Phi	Φ	φ
Kappa	K	κ	Chi	X	χ
Lambda	Λ	λ	Psi	Ψ	ψ
Mu	M	μ	Omega	Ω	ω

Notice that the first two letters are alpha and beta, which are where the word "alphabet" comes from when the two words are combined.

THE SEVEN WONDERS

There were many wonders in the ancient world, and those that the ancients regarded as the most amazing are known as the Seven Wonders of the Ancient World. Sadly, only one is still standing today.

1. The Statue of Zeus at Olympia. The statue took a Greek sculptor, named Phidias, eight years to complete. It was nearly 39 feet (12 m) tall and stood in Zeus's temple at Olympia. It showed him sitting on his throne, and it was decorated with gold, precious stones, and ivory.

VII WONDERS THEME PARK

2. The Temple of Artemis at Ephesus. This huge temple, in what is now Turkey, was decorated with beautiful works of art. It was so magnificent that Philon of Byzantium, who had seen all the other wonders, wrote that when he saw the temple, "all these other wonders were put in the shade."

3. The Colossus of Rhodes. The people of the Greek port of Rhodes defeated an invading army and celebrated by building a 105-foot (32-m) tall bronze-and-iron statue of the sun god, Helios. When it was destroyed by an earthquake less than 60 years after it was finished, the citizens of Rhodes decided not to rebuild it, because they thought that the statue may have angered Helios.

4. The Mausoleum of Halicarnassus. This tomb in Turkey was built by Artemisia for her husband, King Mausolus, when he died. She sent for the best artists in the world to decorate it with statues and carvings. Artemisia died before the building was complete and was placed next to her husband.

5. The Hanging Gardens of Babylon. The gardens, in what is now Iraq, were said to be full of exotic trees, plants, and flowers, arranged on high platforms. It is said the gardens were built by King Nebuchadnezzar as a gift for his wife.

6. The Pyramids of Giza. The three pyramids were each built to hold the body of an Egyptian king (Khufu, Khafre, and Menkaure). The Great Pyramid of Khufu needed 2,300,000 huge stone blocks and took tens of thousands of workers many years to complete. Despite being roughly 4,500 years old, the pyramids are the only wonder you can still see today.

7. The Pharos of Alexandria. The Pharos was a huge lighthouse, built to guide ships into the Egyptian port of Alexandria. There was a fire constantly burning at the top of a tower that was at least 377 feet (115 m) tall, with a large mirror of polished metal to reflect the light across the sea.

MYTHOLOGICALLY
SPEAKING

The ancient Greeks worshipped hundreds of gods and god-desses. They believed that the gods lived on Mount Olympus, which they thought linked Earth to Heaven. Later the Romans often gave Greek gods Roman names and worshipped them, too. Gods and goddesses could stand for different things and really didn't behave very well. Here are just a few, followed by some stories about them.

Greek God	Roman God	Role
Zeus	Jupiter	Sky god and ruler of all the other gods—his weapon was a thunderbolt.
Hera	Juno	Zeus's wife, and goddess of marriage, known for being angry and jealous because Zeus often betrayed her.
Hades	Pluto	God of the underworld.
Apollo	Apollo	Son of Zeus and god of healing and music, as well as lots of other things.
Artemis	Diana	Goddess of hunting and wild animals, twin sister of Apollo.
Ares	Mars	God of war—in Greek stories he was thoughtlessly violent but was much more likeable in Roman versions.
Aphrodite	Venus	Goddess of love and beauty.
Hermes	Mercury	The messenger of the gods with winged sandals, he was thought to bring luck to and protect travelers.
Athena	Minerva	Goddess of war and wisdom (and handi-crafts). Her symbol was the owl.
Hephaestus	Vulcan	God of fire and craftsman for the gods who used volcanoes (which are named after him) to forge weapons.
Poseidon	Neptune	God of the sea.
Persephone	Proserpina	Daughter of Zeus and Demeter (goddess of the harvest).

Persephone

Lots of myths were told to help explain how the world worked. For example, the story of Persephone describes the changing of the seasons. She was the daughter of Zeus and Demeter. Hades, god of the underworld, wished to marry Persephone, but her mother wouldn't let him, so Hades kidnapped Persephone. Demeter was so angry that, as goddess of the harvest, she refused to let crops grow, threatening to starve the human race to death.

Zeus sent the messenger Hermes to force Hades to release Persephone. He agreed, but gave her a pomegranate before she left. Persephone was not allowed to eat food in the underworld, so after eating only one seed, she was forced to spend a third of every year in the underworld. Demeter would become so sad during this time each year that winter came and crops did not grow.

Daedalus and Icarus

Daedalus, who was an inventor and architect, was asked to build a labyrinth (or maze) for King Minos of Crete. Since Daedalus knew how to escape the labyrinth, he was not allowed to leave the island. To get away, he made a pair of wings for himself and his son, Icarus, by joining feathers together with wax. Icarus was thrilled. He flew higher and higher until he was too close to the sun. The heat melted the wax, causing him to plummet to his death in the sea below.

I TOLD YOU SO! YOU NEVER LISTEN TO ME.

Sisyphus

Sisyphus certainly knew how to annoy the gods. One day he betrayed Zeus and was supposed to be punished with death. However, instead of dying, when Hades came to take him to the underworld, Sisyphus took Hades prisoner.

While Hades was trapped, no one in the world could die. Hades was rescued by Ares, and together they made sure that Sisyphus got to the underworld this time. However, Sisyphus was sneaky and escaped death again. This time Zeus sent Hermes to fetch him, and Sisyphus was condemned to push a huge rock up a hill forever. As soon as he'd get near the top, the rock would roll back down to the bottom and Sisyphus had to begin pushing all over again.

Pandora

Zeus was very angry at the titan Prometheus for stealing fire from the gods, so he sought revenge by making a beautiful woman named Pandora (which means all gifts). Zeus sent Pandora down to Earth and gave her as a present to Prometheus's brother, Epimetheus. Zeus told Epimetheus that he should marry Pandora, and he sent Pandora with a sealed pottery vase with instructions never to open it. Pandora was very curious about what was in it. Time and again, she begged Epimetheus to let her open the vase, but he always said no. Finally one day, when he was sleeping, she broke the seal and opened it up.

Suddenly, out flew every kind of trouble that people had never known about before, such as sickness, worry, hate, and envy. The bad things all began to fly away like little bugs, all over the place. Pandora, very sorry now that she had opened the vase, tried to catch the bad things and put them back inside, but it was too late. They all flew away. The very last thing to fly out was hope, which Zeus had sent to keep people going when bad things get them down.

Heracles

From an early age Heracles*, a warrior and half god, was harassed by Hera, Zeus's wife. She hated him because Zeus was his father. She even sent two snakes to try to kill him when he was a baby. However, young Heracles was so strong that he strangled them both.

Instead of killing him, Hera tormented Heracles and drove him so mad that he killed his own wife and children. The Oracle at Delphi told Heracles that to make amends for the murders, he must serve King Eurystheus and perform any task set for him. With Hera's help King Eurystheus came up with a series of what seemed to be impossible tasks, known as the "Labors of Heracles" (see opposite).

Heracles was a true hero, however, and completed all the tasks. He continued to have adventures until he died, poisoned by the blood of a centaur (a creature that is half man and half horse). Here are the tasks Heracles was given:

*The Roman name for the Greek demigod Heracles is Hercules, son of Jupiter, the Roman equivalent of Zeus.

LABORS OF HERACLES

1. TO KILL AND SKIN
THE NEMEAN LION

2. TO SLAY THE
NINE-HEADED
MONSTER, HYDRA

3. TO CATCH THE SACRED
AND SWIFT-RUNNING
ARCADIAN HIND (DEER)

4. TO CAPTURE THE
FLESH-EATING
ERYMANTHIAN BOAR

5. TO CLEAN THE OVER-
FLOWING CATTLE STABLES
OF KING AUGEAS

6. TO DEFEAT THE
MAN-EATING
STYMPHALIAN BIRDS

7. TO CAPTURE THE
FIRE-BREATHING
CRETAN BULL

8. TO CATCH THE MARES
OF KING DIOMEDES—
FLESH-EATING HORSES

9. TO BRING EURYSTHEUS
THE GOLDEN BELT OF
HIPPOLYTE, QUEEN OF THE
FIERCE FEMALE AMAZON
WARRIORS

10. TO STEAL THE CATTLE
OF GERYON, THE STRONGEST
MAN IN THE WORLD

11. TO STEAL THE GOLDEN
APPLES OF IMMORTALITY
FROM THE HESPERIDES,
DAUGHTERS OF THE GOD
ATLAS

12. TO DESCEND INTO THE
UNDERWORLD AND CAPTURE
THE MANY-HEADED GUARD
DOG, CERBERUS

HISTORY STUFF

THE U.S. PRESIDENTS

There have been 43 presidents since George Washington was elected in February 1789. Grover Cleveland was both the 22nd and 24th president—the only one to have served two separate terms in office with another president in between. Below is a list of every U.S. president so far, with the dates of their time spent in office. You will find more detail on the presidents whose names are written in **bold** on the next few pages.

THE GREAT SEAL OF THE UNITED STATES

1	**George Washington**	1789–1797
2	John Adams	1797–1801
3	**Thomas Jefferson**	1801–1809
4	James Madison	1809–1817
5	James Monroe	1817–1825
6	John Quincy Adams	1825–1829
7	Andrew Jackson	1829–1837
8	Martin Van Buren	1837–1841
9	William Henry Harrison *	1841
10	John Tyler	1841–1845
11	James K. Polk	1845–1849
12	Zachary Taylor	1849–1850
13	Millard Fillmore	1850–1853
14	Franklin Pierce	1853–1857
15	James Buchanan	1857–1861
16	**Abraham Lincoln** **	1861–1865
17	Andrew Johnson	1865–1869
18	Ulysses S. Grant	1869–1877
19	Rutherford B. Hayes	1877–1881
20	James A. Garfield **	1881
22	Chester A. Arthur	1881–1885
23	Grover Cleveland	1885–1889

23	Benjamin Harrison	1889–1893
24	Grover Cleveland	1893–1897
25	William McKinley **	1897–1901
26	Theodore Roosevelt	1901–1909
27	William H. Taft	1909–1913
28	**Woodrow Wilson**	1913–1921
29	Warren G. Harding	1921–1923
30	Calvin Coolidge	1923–1929
31	Herbert C. Hoover	1929–1933
32	**Franklin D. Roosevelt** *	1933–1945
33	Harry S. Truman	1945–1953
34	Dwight D. Eisenhower	1953–1961
35	**John F. Kennedy** **	1961–1963
36	Lyndon B. Johnson	1963–1969
37	**Richard Nixon**	1969–1974
38	Gerald Ford	1974–1977
39	Jimmy Carter	1977–1981
40	Ronald Reagan	1981–1989
41	George H. W. Bush	1989–1993
42	Bill Clinton	1993–2001
43	George W. Bush	2001–2009
44	**Barack Obama**	from 2009

* Died in office ** Assassinated

George Washington

Washington was commander-in-chief of the forces rebelling against British rule in the 1770s, known as the American Revolution. He later became leader of the Constitutional Convention, an organization that decided how America should be run. He was elected as the first president of the United States. After serving two four-year terms, he chose not to stay on. This began the tradition that no president may spend more than eight years in office. The only exception to this is Franklin D. Roosevelt (see opposite).

Thomas Jefferson

Jefferson wrote much of the U.S. Declaration of Independence, which states why the first 13 states split from British rule. One of his most recognizable lines says that "all men are created equal" and that their rights should include "life, liberty and the pursuit of happiness." Congress approved the declaration on July 4, 1776, which is still celebrated as Independence Day. The American Revolution was eventually won seven years later.

Abraham Lincoln

When Lincoln was elected, seven pro-slavery Southern states who opposed him left the Union (of states) before his inauguration (when a President is sworn into office). Civil war broke out and four more states joined the South, forming the Confederate States of America. In 1862 Lincoln signed the Emancipation Proclamation (an official announcement freeing slaves), which declared it illegal for anyone in the Confederate States to own slaves. Then, in 1863, Lincoln gave one of the shortest and most famous speeches of all time: the Gettysburg Address. This reminded people that their efforts in the war were for "government of the people, by the people, for the people." Lincoln led the North to victory in 1865, but just

five days after the war ended, a supporter of slavery named John Wilkes Booth shot and killed him. Slavery was officially abolished for the whole country later that year, with the 13th Amendment to the U.S. constitution.

Woodrow Wilson

Wilson led America through the First World War and, at the end of the war, supported the League of Nations. This was an organization set up to encourage countries to cooperate with one another. He was awarded the Nobel Peace Prize for his work. Wilson also passed a number of important laws while in office, including banning child labor and giving women the right to vote.

Franklin D. Roosevelt

Franklin Delano Roosevelt (known as FDR, for short) is the only president elected to office four times. He led the United States through some very difficult years. During a period called the Great Depression, when millions of Americans lost their jobs and suffered terrible poverty, Roosevelt introduced the "New Deal," a program to tackle poor conditions. It helped businesses and those who had lost their jobs. After the Japanese bombed Pearl Harbor in 1941, Roosevelt led America through the Second World War, but he suffered from ill health toward the end of the war and died on April 12, 1945.

John F. Kennedy

At the age of just 43, Kennedy was America's youngest ever president. During his brief time in office, he pledged that the United States would send a man to the moon by the end of the 1960s (which they did in 1969). In October 1962 he dealt with an incident called the Cuban Missile Crisis, when the world came close to nuclear war (see page 71). Kennedy was very popular. However, on November 22, 1963, he was shot by a man named Lee Harvey Oswald while riding through Dallas, Texas, in an open-topped car.

Richard Nixon

Nixon was the first American president to resign. He was involved in the Watergate Scandal, in which five men were hired by Nixon's own political party to burgle their opponent's headquarters in the Watergate building, in Washington, D.C. Things got worse when Nixon tried to cover up the scandal, so he resigned.

Barack Obama

Barack Obama is the first African American to be elected president of the United States and, at just 47 at the time of his inauguration, one of the youngest. His campaign was based on the promise to bring about change for Americans. He came into his presidency facing many challenges, such as the most serious financial crisis in decades, following the collapse of world financial markets in 2008. He also spends much of his time trying to resolve the issues in Afghanistan and Iraq and to find a solution to America's military involvement there.

CLASSIFIED

Two of the most secret operations in history took place during the Second World War.

Top Secret

Station X. During the Second World War, Hitler's Germany had a code-making machine named Enigma. The chance of anyone cracking its codes were one in 150 million million million. A group of some of the brainiest people in Britain gathered at Station X, an English stately home called Bletchley Park, where they worked day and night and successfully decrypted several of the codes of the Axis countries. Their work was vital in helping the Allies (Britain, the United States, the Soviet Union, and other countries) and meant that they could identify enemy plans in advance. Although thousands of people worked at Station X, not one person gave away its secrets. It wasn't until many years later that the importance of Bletchley Park became known.

The Manhattan Project. In 1939 the famous scientist Albert Einstein wrote to President Roosevelt about the importance of atomic research. In 1941 Roosevelt ordered the research to begin. It is known as the Manhattan Project because a lot of the first research was done at Columbia University, in Manhattan. A scientist named Robert Oppenheimer was later put in charge of the main laboratory, which was code-named Project Y.

As a result, the atomic bomb was developed, and two were dropped on the Japanese cities of Nagasaki and Hiroshima in August 1945. This dealt the deciding blow for the United States against Japan in the Second World War. The Japanese surrendered, ending the war. Both cities were destroyed, and over 200,000 people died by the end of that year.

HOW COLD IS A COLD WAR?

In 1946 Winston Churchill spoke of an "iron curtain" falling across Europe. He was referring to what eventually became known as the Cold War.

At the end of the Second World War, the victorious allied countries split into opposing sides. In Eastern Europe, Russia and 14 other communist states made up the Soviet Union. Western Europe, Britain, and the United States were known as the West, and in 1949 they created the North Atlantic Treaty Organization, known as NATO. The Soviets placed pro-Soviet governments in power in Eastern Europe, and in 1955 they formed a military alliance with these countries, which became known as the Warsaw Pact. They agreed to unite to defend themselves against the West.

East and West never actually declared war on each other, but both sides had enough nuclear weapons to destroy the world. There was a great deal of tension for many years. In 1962, when the Soviets placed missiles in Cuba, close to the United States, the world was on the brink of war for almost two weeks before the Soviets agreed to withdraw the missiles.

In the 1980s Mikhail Gorbachev, who was then president of the Soviet Union, introduced reforms. Eastern Europe began to break free from Soviet control. An event that particularly signaled the end of the Cold War was the destruction of the Berlin Wall—a wall built around West Berlin to separate it from communist East Berlin. For nearly 30 years the wall stood as the symbol of the iron curtain, dividing East from West.

BRITISH KINGS AND QUEENS

Here are Britain's kings and queens, with the dates of their reign, starting with Alfred the Great back in the 9th century when England was divided into several different kingdoms.

Alfred the Great	871–899	Henry VI	1422–1461, 1470–1471
Edward the Elder	899–924	Edward IV	1461–1470, 1471–1483
Athelstan	924–939	Edward V	1483
Edmund the Magnificent	939–946	Richard III Crookback	1483–1485
Eadred	946–955	Henry VII Tudor	1485–1509
Eadwig (or Edwy) the Fair	955–959	Henry VIII	1509–1547
Edgar the Peacemaker	959–975	Edward VI	1547–1553
Edward the Martyr	975–978	Lady Jane Grey	1553
Aethelred the Unready	978–1016	Mary I Tudor	1553–1558
Swein Forkbeard	1013	Elizabeth I	1558–1603
Edmund Ironside	1016	James I	1603–1625
Canute the Great	1016–1035	Charles I	1625–1649
Harold Harefoot	1035–1040	Oliver Cromwell *	1653–1658
Hardicanute	1040–1042	Richard Cromwell **	1658–1659
Edward the Confessor	1042–1066	Charles II	1660–1685
Harold II	·1066	James II	1685–1688
William I the Conqueror	1066–1087	William III, Mary II †	1689–1702
William II 'Rufus'	1087–1100	Anne	1702–1714
Henry I Beauclerc	1100–1135	George I	1714–1727
Stephen	1135–1154	George II	1727–1760
Henry II Curtmantle	1154–1189	George III	1760–1820
Richard I the Lionheart	1189–1199	George IV	1820–1830
John Lackland	1199–1216	William IV	1830–1837
Henry III	1216–1272	Victoria	1837–1901
Edward I Longshanks	1272–1307	Edward VII	1901–1910
Edward II	1307–1327	George V	1910–1936
Edward III	1327–1377	Edward VIII	1936
Richard II	1377–1399	George VI	1936–1952
Henry IV Bolingbroke	1399–1413	Elizabeth II	from 1952
Henry V	1413–1422		

* Between 1649 and 1653, following the English Civil War, Britain had no head of state. Cromwell ruled England as Lord Protector from 1653.

** Oliver Cromwell's son ruled England briefly after his father died, until Charles II was invited to be king.

† Ruled jointly until Mary's death in 1694.

IN SEARCH OF CONQUEST

Throughout history countries all over the world have looked to expand their lands by conquering other people's.

Conquerors and Invaders

The Crusades. In the 11th century, Muslim forces captured the holy city of Jerusalem. In response, the Pope launched a series of holy wars against them, known as the Crusades. These continued over the next 200 years. There was even a Children's Crusade, where thousands of young children set out for Jerusalem. Arriving at the French port of Marseilles, they set sail for the Holy Land, only to be captured and sold into slavery.

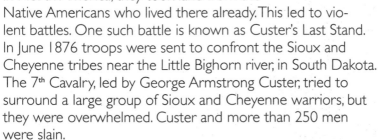

Genghis Khan. In the 13th century, Genghis united the tribes of Mongolia, in east Asia. He led an army of fierce nomadic tribesmen on a violent trail of conquest through northern China, Russia, and Eastern Europe. Each time Genghis conquered a kingdom, the defeated soldiers joined him, so his army grew larger and larger.

North America. When Europeans settled in North America, they took land from the Native Americans who lived there already. This led to violent battles. One such battle is known as Custer's Last Stand. In June 1876 troops were sent to confront the Sioux and Cheyenne tribes near the Little Bighorn river, in South Dakota. The 7th Cavalry, led by George Armstrong Custer, tried to surround a large group of Sioux and Cheyenne warriors, but they were overwhelmed. Custer and more than 250 men were slain.

EXPLORING THE GLOBE

From the beginning of history, people have wondered what was over the next hill or across the ocean, and some people set off to find out.

A Few Great Explorers

Early Explorers. As early as the 4th century b.c., a Greek man named Pytheas explored northwestern Europe. He may even have reached the Arctic Circle. In the 11th century, a Viking, Leif Erikson, reached America. Marco Polo, a Venetian explorer, arrived at the court of the great Kublai Khan, in China, in 1266. His book, *Travels of Marco Polo*, made him one of the most famous explorers of all time.

Christopher Columbus. In 1492 an Italian named Christopher Columbus tried to reach Asia by sailing west around the world rather than east. Instead of reaching Asia, he discovered the New World—Cuba, the Bahamas, Jamaica, and Hispaniola (now Haiti and the Dominican Republic).

Cook and Livingstone. Englishman James Cook (later made a captain) discovered New Zealand in 1769 and Australia a year later. In the 1850s the Scottish explorer Dr. Livingstone became the first European to cross Africa. He found the Zambezi River in 1851 and, in 1855, was the first European to see Zambezi's Victoria Falls.

TROUBLED TIMES

When groups within one country fight each other, it is called a civil war. In the case of one group overthrowing the government, it is known as a revolution.

Civil Wars And Revolutions

English Civil War. In 1642 war broke out between supporters of King Charles I and those who thought the country should be ruled by Parliament. The Royalists (on the side of Charles I) finally surrendered. The King escaped but was captured and later beheaded. Four years after Charles's execution, a man named Oliver Cromwell ruled England with the title Lord Protector.

French Revolution. On July 14, 1789, the people of Paris stormed the Bastille prison and freed its prisoners. This began a revolution that led to the beheading of the French king, Louis XVI. Thousands were beheaded by guillotine during a period known as the Reign of Terror, and France then became a republic (ruled by the people).

Russian Revolution. The First World War caused great poverty in Russia, and in 1917 a group of people called the Bolsheviks, led by a man named Lenin, rose against Tsar Nicholas II, the Russian ruler. They seized power and formed the Union of Soviet Socialist Republics, which they intended to be run by ordinary working people. In reality, however, life remained hard and the Russian people had little freedom.

75

IN TIMES OF WAR

As well as fighting between themselves, many countries have fallen out with one another, too.

Some Rather Important Wars

The Napoleonic Wars. Napoleon Bonaparte led France into a series of battles against its European neighbors until France dominated Europe. However, in 1812 Napoleon invaded Russia. The harsh Russian winter forced him to retreat, and he lost most of his army. Napoleon was exiled in 1814, but he returned to power only to be defeated at the Battle of Waterloo. In 1815 he was exiled again.

The First World War. Beginning in 1914, with Germany and Austria fighting Britain, France, and Russia, this war spread from Europe to involve countries across the world. It was the first modern war—with machine guns, poison gas, tanks, and planes. Hundreds of thousands of men were killed in horrific battles, including those at the Somme and Verdun, in France, and at Passchendaele and Ypres, in Belgium. In 1918 Germany surrendered.

The Second World War. The rise of the dictator Adolf Hitler and the Nazis (an extreme political party) led Germany into war again. World War II was a major turning point in world history, and at this time it involved the largest armed forces, the longest battle lines, and the most destructive weapons of any war.

Hitler wanted to be able to rule all of Europe. He also wanted to eliminate everyone he considered inferior, which he believed included Jews. With Hitler as the leader, Germany began to take over countries and occupy them. Part of his thinking also stemmed from World War I. Most Germans believed that the territory taken from them was taken unfairly. Hitler was able to get a lot of people to conform, but not all people agreed with his Nazi plans.

In 1939 Hitler invaded Poland, so Britain and France declared war on Germany. Many more countries became involved, including the United States and Japan, before the war ended in 1945. The Second World War is known for two especially terrible events. During the war, 6 million Jews were murdered by the Nazis in what is known as the Holocaust. In 1945 two atomic bombs were dropped on cities in Japan, causing great destruction (see page 70).

GEOGRAPHY STUFF

COUNTRIES, CONTINENTS, AND CAPITAL CITIES

You already know that the world is divided into separate areas called countries. But did you know that the number, size, and shape of these areas haven't always been the same? The borders between countries have often been decided through war or political upheaval. A change in government may mean that two countries become a single country—for example, East and West Germany became just Germany in 1990. Or it can mean that one country is divided into smaller countries—Slovakia and the Czech Republic used to be just Czechoslovakia, for example.

Each country has a capital city—usually the largest city in the country—where the government meets to conduct official business. Exceptions to this rule include Tanzania, where the official capital has been Dodoma since 1996, but much of the government still meets in Dar es Salaam, the former capital.

HEY, THEY'VE JUST DISCOVERED AMERICA!

Here is a list of all the countries of the world and their capital cities, divided by continent. The island countries of the Caribbean and those countries in Central America (the thin piece of land linking North and South America) have been listed separately to make them easier to find on a map—in fact, they belong with North America.

Africa

Country	Capital	Country	Capital
Algeria	**Algiers**	Liberia	**Monrovia**
Angola	**Luanda**	Libya	**Tripoli**
Benin	**Porto-Novo**	Madagascar	**Antananarivo**
Botswana	**Gaborone**	Malawi	**Lilongwe**
Burkina Faso	**Ouagadougou**	Mali	**Bamako**
Burundi	**Bujumbura**	Mauritania	**Nouakchott**
Cameroon	**Yaoundé**	Mauritius	**Port Louis**
Cape Verde	**Praia**	Morocco	**Rabat**
Central African Republic	**Bangui**	Mozambique	**Maputo**
Chad	**N'Djamena**	Namibia	**Windhoek**
Comoros	**Moroni**	Niger	**Niamey**
Congo	**Brazzaville**	Nigeria	**Abuja**
(officially Republic		Rwanda	**Kigali**
of the Congo)		São Tomé and Príncipe	**São Tomé**
Congo	**Kinshasa**	Senegal	**Dakar**
(Democratic Republic		Seychelles	**Victoria**
of the Congo)		Sierra Leone	**Freetown**
Côte D'Ivoire	**Yamoussoukro** [1]	Somalia	**Mogadishu**
(formerly Ivory Coast)	**Abidjan** [2]	South Africa	**Pretoria** [3]
Djibouti	**Djibouti**		**Bloemfontain** [4]
Egypt	**Cairo**		**Cape Town** [5]
Equatorial Guinea	**Malabo**	South Sudan	**Juba**
Eritrea	**Asmara**	Sudan	**Khartoum**
Ethiopia	**Addis Ababa**	Swaziland	**Mbabane**
Gabon	**Libreville**	Tanzania	**Dodoma** ‡
Gambia, The	**Banjul**		**Dar es Salaam** ‡‡
Ghana	**Accra**	Togo	**Lomé**
Guinea	**Conakry**	Tunisia	**Tunis**
Guinea-Bissau	**Bissau**	Uganda	**Kampala**
Kenya	**Nairobi**	Zambia	**Lusaka**
Lesotho	**Maseru**	Zimbabwe	**Harare**

[1] Official capital

[2] "De facto" capital, meaning the unofficial center of government

[3] Executive capital, where the laws are carried out

[4] Judicial capital, where the country's judges sit and trials are held

[5] Legislative capital, where laws are made

‡ Official capital ‡‡ Former capital, where parts of the government are still located

Asia

Country	Capital	Country	Capital
Afghanistan	Kabul	Mongolia	Ulaanbaatar
Armenia	Yerevan	Myanmar	Nay Pyi Taw
Azerbaijan	Baku	*(formerly Burma)*	
Bahrain	Manama	Nepal	Kathmandu
Bangladesh	Dhaka	North Korea	Pyongyang
Bhutan	Thimphu	Oman	Muscat
Brunei	Bandar Seri Begawan	Pakistan	Islamabad
		Philippines	Manila
Cambodia	Phnom Penh	Qatar	Doha
China	Beijing	Russia	Moscow
East Timor	Dili	*(Russian Federation)*	*(also Europe)*
(officially Democratic		Saudi Arabia	Riyadh
Republic of Timor-Leste)		Singapore	Singapore
Georgia	Tbilisi	South Korea	Seoul
India	New Delhi	Sri Lanka	Colombo *
Indonesia	Jakarta		Sri Jayawardenepura **
Iran	Tehran	Syria	Damascus
Iraq	Baghdad	Taiwan	Taipei
Israel	Jerusalem	Tajikistan	Dushanbe
Japan	Tokyo	Thailand	Bangkok
Jordan	Amman	Turkey	Ankara
Kazakhstan	Astana		*(also Europe)*
Kuwait	Kuwait City	Turkmenistan	Ashgabat
Kyrgyzstan	Bishkek	United Arab Emirates	Abu Dhabi
Laos	Vientiane	Uzbekistan	Tashkent
Lebanon	Beirut	Vietnam	Hanoi
Malaysia	Kuala Lumpur	Yemen	Sanaa
Maldives	Male		

* Executive capital, where the laws are carried out

** Legislative and judicial capital, where laws are made, the country's judges sit, and trials are held

Europe

Country	Capital	Country	Capital
Albania	Tirana	Luxembourg	Luxembourg
Andorra	Andorra la Vella	Macedonia	Skopje
Austria	Vienna	Malta	Valletta
Belarus	Minsk	Moldova	Chisinau
Belgium	Brussels	Monaco	Monaco
Bosnia and Herzegovina	Sarajevo	Montenegro	Podgorica
Bulgaria	Sofia	Netherlands	Amsterdam *
Croatia	Zagreb		The Hague
Cyprus	Nicosia	Norway	Oslo
Czech Republic	Prague	Poland	Warsaw
Denmark	Copenhagen	Portugal	Lisbon
Estonia	Tallinn	Romania	Bucharest
Finland	Helsinki	Russia	Moscow
France	Paris	*(Russian Federation)*	*(also Asia)*
Germany	Berlin	San Marino	San Marino
Greece	Athens	Serbia	Belgrade
Hungary	Budapest	Slovakia	Bratislava
Iceland	Reykjavik	Slovenia	Ljubljana
Ireland	Dublin	Spain	Madrid
Italy	Rome	Sweden	Stockholm
Kosovo	Pristina	Switzerland	Bern
(declared itself independent, 2008)		Turkey	Ankara *(also Asia)*
Latvia	Riga	Ukraine	Kiev
Liechtenstein	Vaduz	United Kingdom	London
Lithuania	Vilnius	Vatican City	Vatican City

Oceania

Country	Capital	Country	Capital
Australia	Canberra	Palau	Melekeok
Fiji	Suva	Papua	Port Moresby
Kiribati	Bairiki	New Guinea	
Marshall Islands	Majuro	Samoa	Apia
Micronesia *(Federated*	Palikir	Solomon Islands	Honiara
States of Micronesia)		Tonga	Nuku'alofa
Nauru	Yaren	Tuvalu	Funafuti
New Zealand	Wellington	Vanuatu	Port Vila

* Official capital, where the laws are carried out

Central America and the Caribbean

Country	Capital	Country	Capital
Antigua and Barbuda	St John's	Haiti	Port-au-Prince
Bahamas, The	Nassau	Honduras	Tegucigalpa
Barbados	Bridgetown	Jamaica	Kingston
Belize	Belmopan	Nicaragua	Managua
Costa Rica	San José	Panama	Panama City
Cuba	Havana	Saint Kitts and Nevis	Basseterre
Dominica	Roseau	Saint Lucia	Castries
Dominican Republic	Santo Domingo	Saint Vincent and	Kingstown
El Salvador	San Salvador	the Grenadines	
Grenada	Saint George's	Trinidad	Port of Spain
Guatemala	Guatemala City	and Tobago	

North America

Country	Capital	Country	Capital
Canada	Ottawa	United States	Washington, D.C.
Mexico	Mexico City		

South America

Country	Capital	Country	Capital
Argentina	Buenos Aires	Guyana	Georgetown
Bolivia	La Paz *	Paraguay	Asunción
	Sucre **	Peru	Lima
Brazil	Brasilia	Suriname	Paramaribo
Chile	Santiago	Uruguay	Montevideo
Colombia	Bogotá	Venezuela	Caracas
Ecuador	Quito		

* Administrative capital, where the main government is run

** Judicial capital, where the country's judges sit and trials are held

THE UNITED STATES

The Journey from 13 to 50

On July 4, 1776, the Declaration of Independence was signed, officially declaring the United States independent from the Kingdom of Great Britain. At that time, the United States consisted of 13 colonies. In 1794 two more states joined the Union, and the United States continued to grow until 1959, when Alaska and Hawaii became the last two states to join. The American flag has 50 stars on it to represent the 50 states, and there are 13 red and white stripes, representing the original 13 colonies. Below are the names of the 50 states and their capital cities.

State	Capital	State	Capital
Alabama	Montgomery	Montana	Helena
Alaska	Juneau	Nebraska	Lincoln
Arizona	Phoenix	Nevada	Carson City
Arkansas	Little Rock	New Hampshire *	Concord
California	Sacramento	New Jersey *	Trenton
Colorado	Denver	New Mexico	Santa Fe
Connecticut *	Hartford	New York *	Albany
Delaware *	Dover	North Carolina *	Raleigh
Florida	Tallahassee	North Dakota	Bismarck
Georgia *	Atlanta	Ohio	Columbus
Hawaii	Honolulu	Oklahoma	Oklahoma City
Idaho	Boise	Oregon	Salem
Illinois	Springfield	Pennsylvania *	Harrisburg
Indiana	Indianapolis	Rhode Island *	Providence
Iowa	Des Moines	South Carolina *	Columbia
Kansas	Topeka	South Dakota	Pierre
Kentucky	Frankfort	Tennessee	Nashville
Louisiana	Baton Rouge	Texas	Austin
Maine	Augusta	Utah	Salt Lake City
Maryland *	Annapolis	Vermont	Montpelier
Massachusetts *	Boston	Virginia *	Richmond
Michigan	Lansing	Washington	Olympia
Minnesota	St. Paul	West Virginia	Charleston
Mississippi	Jackson	Wisconsin	Madison
Missouri	Jefferson City	Wyoming	Cheyenne

*The 13 colonies along the East Coast of the North American continent, where Europeans first settled in the 16th century

TALLEST, LARGEST, LONGEST

Who isn't interested in knowing the tallest, largest, longest of anything they can possibly imagine? The largest bird? The ostrich. The tallest building? The Taipei 101 in Taiwan. The longest railway? The Trans-Siberian. The list goes on. But since we're talking geography here, let's explore the tallest mountains, largest oceans, and longest rivers.

Record-Breaking World

Mountains. The tallest mountains in the world are all in an area called the Himalayas, in Asia. There are several measuring over 26,250 feet (8,000 m). These include Everest, at 29,028 feet (8,848 m), K2 at 28,257 feet (8,611 m), and Kanchenjunga at (8,598 m) tall.

Outside Asia the tallest mountain is Aconcagua, in Argentina, which is 22,831 feet (6,959 m) high. The tallest in the United States is Mount McKinley in Alaska, at 20,321 feet (6,194 m), while in Africa, Kilimanjaro, in Kenya, tops the charts at 19,340 feet (5,895 m). Mont Blanc, which straddles the borders of France and Italy, is the tallest mountain in Europe, at 15,770 feet (4,807 m).

Mauna Kea, a dormant (resting) volcano in the Hawaiian Islands, deserves a mention, too. Measuring 334,000 feet (10,200 m) from base to top, it's taller than Everest, but only 13,795 feet (4,205 m) of that is above the surface of the sea. The UK's tallest mountain, Ben Nevis in Scotland, is just 4406 feet (1,343 m) high.

Oceans. All oceans are connected, so in a way there is just one big ocean—sometimes called the World Ocean. This is divided into the Pacific at 102.5 million square miles (165.5 million km²), the Atlantic at 51 million square miles (81.5 million km²), the Indian at 46 million square miles (73.5 million km²), and the Arctic 9 million square miles (at 14.1 million km²).

Seas. Areas of water separating two landmasses, often called seas, are also part of one of the main oceans. Some inland salt-water lakes are called seas, too, but aren't really. The largest sea in the world is the South China Sea at 1.8 million square miles (3 million km²). It lies between mainland Asia and the islands of the Philippines and is part of the Pacific Ocean. Next largest is the Caribbean, at 1.7 million square miles (2.8 million km²), which is east of Central America and part of the Atlantic Ocean. The Mediterranean Sea, measuring 1.6 million square miles (2.5 million km²), is also part of the Atlantic, and lies between southern Europe and North Africa. The Bering Sea, at 1.4 million square miles (2.3 million km²), sits between Alaska and Russia and is part of the Pacific. And the Gulf of Mexico, at 932,000 square miles (1.5 million km²), separates the eastern United States and Mexico and is part of the Atlantic (and is a sea).

Rivers. The Nile and the Amazon have been fighting for the title of the world's longest river for years, but measuring a river isn't easy. Deciding where the sea stops and the river starts is one thing, then finding the river's true source (where it rises from the ground) is another. The five longest rivers are the Nile in Egypt, 4,132 miles (6,650 km) long, the Amazon in Brazil, at 4,007 miles (6,450 km), the Yangtze in China, at 3,964 miles (6,380 km), the Mississippi–Missouri in the United States, at 3,740 miles (6,020 km), and Yenisey–Angara in Russia, at 3,448 miles (5,550 km).

The UK's longest river, at a measly 220 miles (354 km), is the Severn, with the Thames hot on its heels at 215 miles (346 km).

HOW LAND IS SHAPED AND CHANGED

Mountains, oceans, and rivers are constantly changing by tiny amounts, but over the 4.6 billion years of the planet's life so far, it adds up to a lot. Here are some reasons for these transformations:

Erosion

Land is worn away by the action of wind and water, which can even change the shape of coastlines. The land doesn't just vanish, though; it gets moved elsewhere. For example, a fast-flowing river picks up gravel from the riverbed, carries it along, and deposits it again where the water slows down.

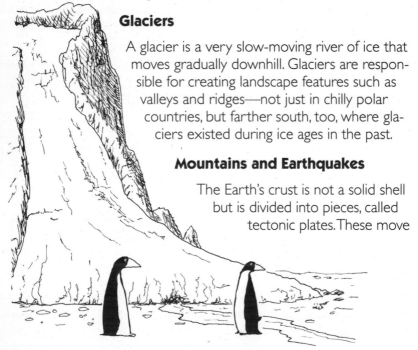

Glaciers

A glacier is a very slow-moving river of ice that moves gradually downhill. Glaciers are responsible for creating landscape features such as valleys and ridges—not just in chilly polar countries, but farther south, too, where glaciers existed during ice ages in the past.

Mountains and Earthquakes

The Earth's crust is not a solid shell but is divided into pieces, called tectonic plates. These move around very slowly, and when they meet, it causes geological events, such as earthquakes, to take place. Many mountain ranges are the result of two plates colliding and pushing the land upward. Everest, in the Himalayas, gets 2.4 inches (6.1 cm) taller each year as two plates push together. Earthquakes occur along boundaries between plates.

Volcanoes

The inside of the planet is far less pleasant than the surface, because it is made of extremely hot melted rock called magma. A volcano is a hole in the Earth's crust that leads to an underground chamber full of magma. They are usually found along the edges of tectonic plates. Most are tall, with craters (holes) in the center. When an eruption occurs, ash and magma escape from the hole and can cause great destruction. The steep sides of a volcano are made of ash and magma from previous eruptions.

Did You Know?

Magma hardens into stone as it cools and can make new land. For instance, the island of Hawaii is actually made of five volcanoes—Kilauea, Mauna Loa, Hualalai, Mauna Kea, and Kohala. The land surrounding the volcanoes formed from the eruptions.

THE WATER CYCLE

Earth is the only place that scientists currently know of in the solar system where liquid water exists. It is continually recycled in a process called the water cycle, shown below:

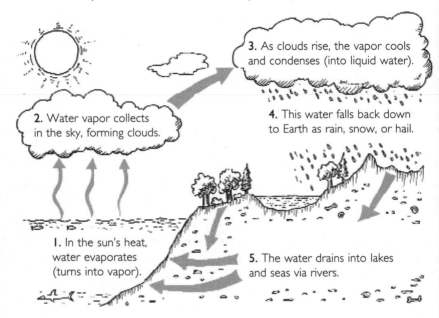

3. As clouds rise, the vapor cools and condenses (into liquid water).

2. Water vapor collects in the sky, forming clouds.

4. This water falls back down to Earth as rain, snow, or hail.

1. In the sun's heat, water evaporates (turns into vapor).

5. The water drains into lakes and seas via rivers.

Droughts

The quantity of water on Earth doesn't change, so it can be difficult to understand why many places don't have enough. In some countries, weather patterns (known as droughts) mean that very little rain falls for long periods of time. This can mean that there is not enough safe fresh water in those areas for people and animals to drink. Often, crops fail to grow, which leads to a shortage of food. Making sure that any available water is safe and doesn't contain disease-causing organisms is expensive and difficult.

WEATHER AND CLIMATE

All of our weather—snow, rain, humidity, and so on—happens just 6 to 10 miles (10 to 16 km) above the Earth's surface in the area of the atmosphere called the troposphere. When news of a blizzard, thunderstorm, heat wave, or cold front is heard, it becomes a big topic of discussion, especially when it might cause schools to be closed! So if you're thinking that meteorology might be in your future—or if you just want to discover how the weather systems work, read on!

Wind, Rain, and Wild Weather

Weather Patterns. Where rain or snow falls depends on the way air moves around above the Earth, which in turn depends on the sun warming the air. Warm air tends to rise. This creates low pressure because the air is pressing down less against the Earth. Clouds form as the water vapor in the air cools and condenses into liquid water. Cooling air sinks, which creates high pressure and fewer clouds. Air tends to try to move from areas of high pressure to areas of low pressure, forming winds. Wind can carry clouds around and cause them to rain far away from where they were formed. The shape of the land affects the speed and direction of winds, and different winds can affect each other.

All of these factors produce the weather, but the process is very complex and chaotic, which is why forecasters are often wrong when they try to predict what might happen more than a few days in advance.

Climate Zones. Even though the weather can be unpredictable, you can be reasonably confident that you'll be warmer in Spain in July than you will in Moscow in January. The Earth is tilted on its axis (the vertical line through its center around which it spins), so parts of it get more sunshine than others at different times of year. This produces seasons. If the planet didn't have this tilt, there would be no seasons anywhere.

At the North and South poles, there are basically two seasons each year—a summer of 24-hour daylight when the pole faces the sun, and a winter of 24-hour darkness when it doesn't, with a very quick changeover. Few plants grow there, and most animals visit only in summer, leaving before winter begins. These areas are called the Polar zones. As you move away from the poles, summer days and winter nights get shorter and the changes between summer and winter get long enough to be called seasons in their own right: spring and autumn. Because of the additional sunlight, plants tend to grow more in spring and summer. Countries with four distinct seasons are found in the temperate zones.

At the equator (the widest part of the Earth between the poles), there is no obvious spring, summer, autumn, or winter. Instead, countries here have a rainy season and a dry season. They are in the tropical zone. Plants and animals often grow and reproduce throughout the year.

Extreme Weather. When areas of low-pressure air form in the middle of high-pressure air, there will often be storms. In heavy rainstorms, electricity is discharged from cloud to cloud or between the land and a cloud, producing lightning. The heat of the lightning passing through the air produces the sound of thunder. The time that passes between seeing the flash and hearing the rumble tells you how close the lightning is—every second equals roughly 2 miles (3 km).

Tornadoes. Tornadoes, caused by spinning funnels of air during thunderstorms, descend to the ground from large clouds. They suck up loose bits and pieces from the ground—these can even include cars and people if a tornado is large enough. Tornados over the sea can result in one of the rarest of all weather phenomenons: raining fish!

HUMAN IMPACT

Inventors, philosophers, doctors, physicists, and many others have made huge strides in the fields of medicine, science, religion, and so on. Think of how different our world would be without Thomas Edison, Albert Einstein, or the Greek philosophers Aristotle and Plato. However, there are other ways people have changed our planet that have not been so positive. . . .

• On the island of Madagascar, so many trees have been removed to make space for crops that hundreds of tons of soil washed away. So much soil, washed down from the hills, built up in the river basin that a port had to be moved to prevent ships from running aground.

• Cattle and other animals bred for meat add to climate change with the gases they emit through their burps and flatulence (no, really!).

• Some of the trash that humans throw away collects together in the ocean. The Great Pacific Garbage Patch, for example, is in fact two huge islands of floating plastic in the eastern and western Pacific Ocean. Together they measure several million square miles.

Did You Know?

Many materials that are used to package food take a huge amount of time to decompose (rot back into the ground). An aluminum soda can, for example, will still be around 100 years from now unless it is recycled. A plastic bag could take up to 1,000 years to decompose.

GEOLOGICAL TIME, IN BRIEF

Scientists believe the Earth was formed 4.6 billion years ago, but geological time is measured from 600 million years ago, with the start of the Palaeozoic era (geological time is divided into eras, then periods, then epochs). This was when the first multicellular (made of more than one cell) plants and animals first appeared, followed by the first primitive arthropods (animals such as insects, with jointed legs) and chordates (animals with spinal cords). At the end of this era, about 95 percent of all marine species became extinct, although a larger proportion of plants and animals on land survived—no one knows exactly why.

The Mesozoic era began 250 million years ago. Chordate animals became established on land, and dinosaurs soon dominated the scene. Mammals and birds also appeared,

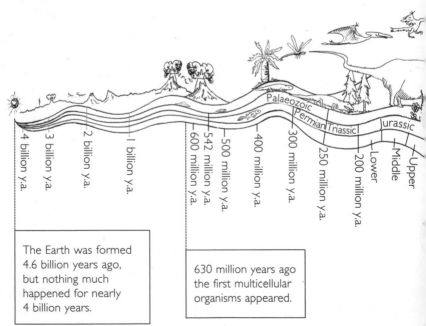

The Earth was formed 4.6 billion years ago, but nothing much happened for nearly 4 billion years.

630 million years ago the first multicellular organisms appeared.

descended from two separate kinds of reptiles. This era is divided into three periods—the Triassic, Jurassic, and Cretaceous. At the end of this era, another mass extinction occurred (perhaps caused by a catastrophe such as a massive asteroid strike or huge volcanic eruption). It wiped out a large proportion of life on the planet, including the dinosaurs, but that did mean there was more room for other mammals to thrive.

The Cenozoic era began 65 million years ago (the planet is still in it now). Mammals took over from dinosaurs, and many new species evolved, including humans, who were first around some 200,000 years ago. There have been seven epochs in this era. The current epoch is the Holocene, but many scientists say that a new epoch should be recognized—the Anthropocene—dating from around the year a.d. 1800 when human impact on the Earth can be noticed.

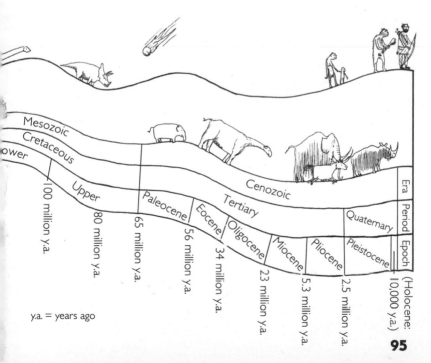

Mesozoic
Cretaceous
ower
100 million y.a.
Upper
80 million y.a.
65 million y.a.
Paleocene
56 million y.a.
Eocene
34 million y.a.
Oligocene
23 million y.a.
Tertiary
Cenozoic
Miocene
5.3 million y.a.
Pliocene
2.5 million y.a.
Pleistocene
Quaternary
10,000 y.a.
(Holocene:

Era
Period
Epoch

y.a. = years ago

95

MATH STUFF

WHAT'S IN A NUMBER?

Math is not only for engineers and accountants. Whether you realize it or not, you use math all the time—to count change, divide your friends up into teams, or to figure out how many songs you can afford to download to your MP3 player, for instance. The basic concept of addition, subtraction, multiplication, and division goes back hundreds of years. But the way we do math today is much different than in Greek and Roman times.

When in Rome

For centuries Roman numerals were widely used for counting and mathematics. They are written using the letters I (1), V (5), X (10), L (50), C (100), D (500), and M (1000). The order the letters are written in tells you what the number is. For example, if you place a lower Roman numeral in front of a larger Roman numeral, it reduces the value of the larger numeral—so CM is 900. If you place a lower Roman numeral *after* a larger numeral, it raises the value of the larger Roman numeral—so XV is 15. Just to write 1915 you'd need to write out MCMXV. Imagine trying to calculate a really complicated math problem!

Number Symbols

The numbers we use now—1, 2, 3, 4, 5, 6, 7, 8, and 9—are called Hindu-Arabic numerals. These symbols developed in India and the surrounding area over several hundred years. Traders going between North Africa and Spain then helped them spread to Europe, and when translations of mathematical writings became available, even more people learned about them. The invention of the printing press in the mid-15th century meant that the symbols became familiar to many more people, and eventually the Hindu-Arabic numerals took over from Roman numerals.

Take 10 Fingers

The decimal system uses 10 (*deci* is from the Latin word *decimus,* meaning 10) as the base for counting. This makes a lot of sense, as people have been counting things on their fingers for thousands of years. It's much more obvious than the Babylonians' base 60 or the Mayans' base 20 systems, for example.

The numbers 1, 2, 3, 4, 5, 6, 7, 8, and 9 are very useful for counting, but the addition of 0 (zero) makes things even simpler. Before zero, if you wanted to keep a record of how many sheep you had, for instance, you might scratch a line on a stick for each one. So if you had three sheep, you'd scratch three lines: III. However, if you were lucky enough to have

300 sheep, things got tricky, because 300 scratches doesn't look much different than 301 scratches. It also takes a lot of space and a lot of scratching, and what if someone interrupted you after the 288th scratch and you lost count?

The decimal system takes only three symbols to write 300, rather than 300 scratches. With zero, you can show just how many sheep you have by the position of the numbers—units, tens, hundreds, thousands, and so on. Each time you move your number to the left (your three sheep, for instance) and tack a zero on the right, you multiply that number by 10. This way, you can quickly and easily write enormous numbers:

3

30

300

3,000

Did You Know?

Only in the last few hundred years have people begun to think of zero as a number. It seems odd now, but math was used mainly for counting *things* for thousands of years. With nothing to count, why would you need a number?

A NUMBER OF QUESTIONS

You probably already know that a number line is very useful for doing simple calculations. You can easily subtract 3 from 5, just by starting on the 5 and moving 3 numbers to the left, to reach 2:

0 1 2 3 4 5 6 7 8 9 10

A number line also leads to interesting questions, such as, What happens to the left of the zero? Where does the line end? or What do the positions between the numbers mean? All these questions have interesting answers.

To the left of zero are negative numbers (numbers less than zero). If you subtract 5 from 3, you'll get a negative number. Just start at 3 and take 5 steps to the left to reach −2 (minus 2):

-10 -9 -8 -7 -6 -5 -4 -3 -2 -1 0 1 2 3 4 5 6 7 8 9 10

The number line doesn't come to an end, either—it goes on forever. The largest number you could think of can always have a one added to it to make it even bigger. To put it another way, the line goes on to infinity, which is written using the ∞ symbol.

Between the numbers on the number line are fractions, which you'll find out more about on page 103.

COMPARE AND CONTRAST

Ratios, fractions, decimals, and percentages are not just useful in math lessons—you'll also find them very handy when you're out shopping, and comparing prices of your favorite video games, for instance.

The Golden Ratio

A ratio compares one thing to another—your eight fingers and two thumbs, for example, mean that your ratio of fingers to thumbs is 8 to 2, written as 8:2. A ratio that pops up regularly is called the golden ratio. It is roughly 8:13. So if you drew a rectangle measuring 3 inches by 5 inches (8 cm by 13 cm), it would have the golden ratio and can be called a "golden rectangle." It can always be divided into a square and another golden rectangle. If you then draw a curve from one corner to the opposite corner on each square, a spiral will begin to appear (right). It appears in the shapes of many books, buildings, paintings, and statues, as people rather like the way that it looks.

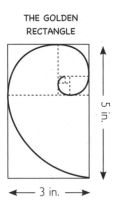

THE GOLDEN
RECTANGLE

5 in.

◄— 3 in. —►

Ratios in Circles

One of the most important ratios you'll come across compares the distance around a circle (the circumference) to the distance across it (the diameter). It is roughly 22:7, or pi, written as π—a symbol from the Greek alphabet. You are most likely to use it to find out the area of a circle using the formula $\pi \times r^2$, where r is the radius of the circle.

Fractions and Decimals

Fractions are the things you get if you divide something into smaller parts. Fractions can often be written as ratios, too. For instance, there are seven times as many days in a year as there are weeks. You could say that a day is one-seventh of a week, which you can write as the fraction ⅐, or the ratio of weeks to days is 1:7.

Decimals are simply fractions written with numbers after a dot called a decimal point. For example, if you put ⅐ into a calculator (by dividing 1 by 7), it will give you the decimal version of one-seventh, which is about 0.142857 going on forever, or "recurring." That means you could carry on writing 0.142857142857142857142857 ... over and over and over. However, to save space (and paper), you could put a line over the recurring section of numbers, like this: 0.$\overline{142857}$.

Some decimals are short and neat, such as a half, which is 0.5 as a decimal. Others are long and neat, like one-third, which is 0.3 (recurring). Then there are the long and messy decimals, such as π(3.14159265…), which has no recurring pattern to the numbers after the decimal point, ever.

WEIRD NUMBERS

Although people came up with counting and mathematics, numbers often appear in the natural world, too. Take odd and even numbers, for instance. Practically every living thing that has legs has either 2, 4, 6, 8 or some other even number. Flowers, on the other hand, very often have an odd number of petals—5 is especially popular (though no one is sure why). Everything you can see is made up of atoms, which come in around 100 different types, called elements, each of which has a particular number of particles called protons (see page 124).

Triangular Numbers

In ancient Greece several men with time on their hands seriously enjoyed talking about numbers (oddly, women weren't allowed to do such things then). What they especially liked was to label numbers according to their shapes. Triangular numbers were a particular favorite.

The number 10 is a triangular number because it can be arranged into a triangle shape (below).

So a triangular number is any number you can arrange in a triangle: 1, 3, 6, 10, 15, 21, and 28 are all triangular numbers. If you arrange each of the numbers in the sequence into triangle shapes, the bottom row of the next number in the sequence will always have one more dot than on the bottom row of the previous triangle in the sequence.

Square and Cube Numbers

More useful to people today are square numbers, where the number can be arranged in a square shape, like 9:

$$\bigcirc \ \bigcirc \ \bigcirc$$
$$\bigcirc \ \bigcirc \ \bigcirc$$
$$\bigcirc \ \bigcirc \ \bigcirc$$

Each side has 3 dots, so you can say that 9 is 3 **squared** (or $3^2 = 9$), and that 3 is the **square root** of 9 (or $\sqrt{9} = 3$). It doesn't stop there either. Imagine the dots are sweets (nice sticky ones) and you build a cube out of them. If the cube is 3 sweets high, 3 sweets wide and 3 sweets deep, it contains 27 sweets, so 27 is 3 **cubed** (or $3^3 = 27$). You can check this number by multiplying 3 three times: $3 \times 3 \times 3 = 27$.

Powers

The little number ^{3} in 3^3 is a **power.** You can have higher powers, too, such as 3^6, or "three to the power of six." It's much trickier (impossible, actually) to build from sweets, but easy enough to work out by multiplying six 3's together: $3^6 = 3 \times 3 \times 3 \times 3 \times 3 \times 3 = 729$.

People who are interested in really BIG numbers use a system that is based on powers of 10. The sun's mass is roughly 2,000,000,000,000,000,000,000,000,000,000 kg, for instance. To save on zeros, this can be written: 2×10^{30} kg, because 10^{30} is the same as 10 multiplied by itself 30 times, which is the same as 1 followed by 30 zeros. This system of writing large numbers is called scientific notation.

MEASURING, TO BE PRECISE

One of the most practical ways to use numbers is for measuring things. Scientists measure most things with what are called SI units (SI stands for *Système International,* which is French for International System). These are a standard set of units that everyone in the world can work from. This means that a kilogram in China, for instance, will be exactly the same as a kilogram in Greenland or Saudi Arabia. There is even a kilogram weight, kept in a vault in Paris, that the weight of all kilograms are based on.

So length is measured in feet, and area is measured in square feet (ft^2) or square meters (m^2), volume is measured in cubic feet (ft^3) or cubic meters (m^3), mass is measured in pounds (lbs) or kilograms (kg), and time is measured in seconds (s).

One of the best things about SI units is that most of them have smaller and larger versions. The different sizes of unit fit together simply, just by multiplying or dividing by 10, 100 or 1,000. For instance, a kilogram can be divided into grams, or multiplied into metric tons. There are 1,000 grams in a kilogram and 1,000 kilograms in a metric ton.

Taking Measures

By whipping out a tape measure, you could discover how tall your mom is. How easy this is depends on both your mom's patience and how exact you want the measurement to be. Measuring to the nearest foot is very easy—maybe she is 5 feet tall. Measuring her height to the nearest inch is much more difficult. If you tried measuring to the nearest centimeter or millimeter, things would get very tricky—as often happens when you try to measure things more exactly than anyone needs. You will suddenly find you need to answer a lot of annoying questions such as, Should I measure to the top of her hairdo? Should she take her socks off? Does her height change when she breathes in? and Is this going to take all day?

The point is, the exactness with which you should make a measurement depends on what you're measuring and why. A flea needs a different unit of measurement than a whale, for instance.

JUMP INTO GEOMETRY

Geometry is the type of math that explores shapes, lines, and angles. Some shapes—circles, for instance—are two dimensional (flat), while others, such as spheres, are three dimensional (solid). Here are a few of the most important two- and three-dimensional shapes and their names:

Of course, geometric shapes are not just interesting to mathematicians. Engineers and architects use triangles when they design things, because they're rigid and strong. Builders stack cuboids (although they would probably call them bricks) to create walls because they fit together nicely without leaving any gaps. Even bees use geometry, building their hives using hexagons, a shape that uses the smallest possible amount of wax to make a very strong structure.

Geometry is useful to scientists, too. For example, the atoms of different crystals are arranged in different patterns, and this affects the crystals' properties, meaning that they have different characteristics. The atoms in a diamond, for example, are arranged in a pattern of interlocking tetrahedrons, and as a result, it is the world's hardest substance. Graphite is made out of exactly the same stuff as diamonds (carbon). However, the atoms in graphite (the stuff in the middle of your pencil) are arranged in layers of interlocking hexagons, so it is one of the softest substances.

Angles

Angles, measured in degrees (°), are an important part of geometry, too. A full circle has 360°, and this goes back to the Babylonians, who lived around 4,000 years ago. They loved numbers that 60 could be divided into. (They're the reason we divide hours into 60 minutes and minutes into 60 seconds.)

Right angles are particularly important in geometry. There are four in every rectangle and square, and a right-angled triangle also has one. A right angle is exactly 90°. Angles that are less than 90° are called **acute** angles. Angles that are more than 90° are **obtuse** and an angle that is more than 180° is called a **reflex angle.**

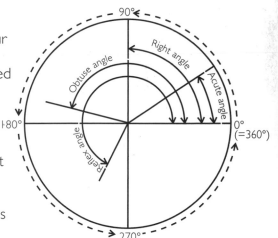

Did You Know?

The angles of the three points of a triangle always add up to 180°, no matter the dimensions of the triangle.

SOME ALGEBRA MAGIC

Algebra is all about using letters (very often x and y) in place of numbers. It's a lot more useful than it sounds. In fact, a lot of scientific discoveries can only be explained with algebra.

For instance, if you fell off a cliff, your speed would gradually increase as the Earth's gravity pulled you toward the ground (or to a nice, safe splashdown in water, hopefully). To while away the journey down, you could work out how fast you are going at any given moment, using a bit of algebra.

You can work out your speed by multiplying the time you have been falling by your acceleration (the rate at which your speed increases). It can be written in an equation like this: s = t x a (speed equals time multiplied by acceleration).

On Earth things accelerate at about (10 m) per second per second. So to find out your speed after 2 seconds, just use the numbers that you know to replace letters in the equation. You know that **t** (time) is 2 (the two seconds that you have been falling), and you know that **a** (acceleration) is 10. So: s = 2 x 10 = (20 m) per second.

Pythagoras's Theorem

Here's a rather nifty equation: $a^2 = b^2 + c^2$. It's called Pythagoras's theorem, and it tells you that in a right-angled triangle, the length of the longest side (the hypotenuse) squared is equal to the lengths of the two shorter sides squared and added together.

For instance, in a right-angled triangle whose shorter sides are 3 cm and 4 cm long, the hypotenuse must be 5 cm long. Here's why:

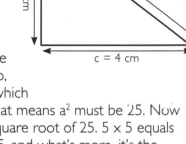

Imagine **b** is 3 cm long and **c** is 4 cm long. If **b** is squared (b^2), then it will be 3^2, or 9. **c** must be squared (c^2), so it is 4^2, or 16, so, $b^2 + c^2$ is the same as 9 + 16, which equals 25. Since $a^2 = b^2 + c^2$, that means a^2 must be 25. Now all you need to do is find the square root of 25. 5 × 5 equals 25, so 5 is the square root of 25, and what's more, it's the length of the hypotenuse, too.

Pythagoras and his followers loved both triangles and numbers. So they were delighted with this theorem, until they noticed what happens if the shorter sides of a triangle are, say, both 2 units long. Then the length of the hypotenuse is the square root of $22 + 22$—in other words the square root of 8, which is 2.828427. Sadly, the Pythagoreans only liked simple numbers, like 1, 2, 3, and so on. They just couldn't cope with messy "irrational" numbers like 2.828427. They found them so upsetting that they tried to keep them a secret—
and even executed one of their friends for talking about them too much.

WHAT ARE THE CHANCES?

Statistics is a very useful kind of math because it allows you to peer into the future. First, you need to collect data (information) about the past and/or the present, after which you have to study it (often by drawing a chart). Then you need to draw some conclusions about what's going on. From this you can make your predictions. Simple!

Say you want to go on vacation to Belgium and avoid the rain. All you need to do is find out how many dry days there were in each of the last 12 months and draw a chart like the one below, called a histogram or bar chart:

So, according to the chart above, the driest month was July.

However, before booking the vacation, you still need to be a little cautious. For instance, you could improve your chances of a good vacation even more by using data from the last 10 years instead of just the last 12 months, but to do that, you need to do some calculations (very easy ones). Here's how:

If, in each January of the last 10 years, the numbers of dry days were: 12, 15, 17, 17, 14, 16, 16, 11, 12, and 16, then you can find the average number of dry days per January by adding the days up and dividing by 10. So 146 ÷ 10 = 14.6. Now you can round that figure up to 15 days. Do that for each month and you can check whether July is still your best bet for a dry vacation. Even then, July is still the most promising month—but you can't be absolutely certain of staying dry. This is where "probability" comes in.

Probability

If you know how probable something is, you can give that probability a number. Something certain, such as Monday following Sunday, has a probability of 1. Something impossible, such as living forever, gets a zero, and anything else that *might* happen, has a number in between.

If you toss a coin, the probability (or chance) of getting heads is 0.5, which you can call a 1 in 2 probability (because the head is one of only two options). You can also call it a 50:50 probability (if you tossed 100 coins, you would get about 50 heads and 50 tails) or a 50% probability.

Unlikely things have small probabilities—the chance of your parents winning the national lottery, for instance, is about 0.00000007, which is about 1 in 14 million.

Did You Know?

How probable is it that two people in the same room have the same birthday? You might expect to need a large group to make it probable, but in fact, just 27 people would do.

MATHEMATICAL GREATS

Throughout history, many people have spent a lot of time thinking about math. Some of them came up with some very useful ideas that we couldn't do without today.

Pythagoras

(Greek, born around 580 b.c., died around 500 b.c.)

Not much is known about Pythagoras, he lived such a long time ago. It is not even certain that he came up with the theorem named after him (see page 111), as his followers liked to give him credit for things (plus they were a very secretive bunch). Pythagoras thought that everything, including music, astronomy, and nature, could be broken down into numbers.

Archimedes

(Greek, born around 287 b.c., died around 212 b.c.)

Archimedes worked out how many grains of sand would fill

the universe, a more accurate value for π (see page 103), and a set of equations that gave the areas and volumes of various shapes. Legend says that he even came up with one theory while he was in the bath, although this is probably not the case. However, he did build war machines to help defend his home city from the Romans, and died during an attack.

Leonardo Fibonacci

(Italian, born around 1170, died around 1250)

Fibonacci described a sequence of numbers in which each number is calculated by adding together the pair of numbers before it (1, 1, 2, 3, 5, 8, 13, 21, 34, and so on). The Fibonacci Sequence, as it's now called, appears naturally in things such as the spiral structures of pineapples, pine cones, and sunflower seeds (the seeds grow in spirals, 21 counterclockwise and 34 clockwise).

Fibonacci also promoted the modern decimal system and Hindu-Arabic numerals (see page 98) and proved how much easier it was to do math with them.

Pierre Fermat

(French, born 1601, died 1665)

Fermat helped to develop theories about probability (see page 113) and made breakthroughs in geometry and the theory of numbers. However, he is probably most famous for jotting down a note in the margin of a book. He wrote that he had solved a particularly tricky problem but didn't have space to note the answer down just then. This baffled many other mathematicians for three centuries, because Fermat never did write down the answer. Finally, with the help of a gigantic computer, an English mathematician and a Canadian physicist were able to work out the solution to the problem Fermat referred to, and published it in 1995.

SCIENCE STUFF

FIRST PHYSICS

Physics studies the universe and what goes on in it. Physicists are especially interested in matter and energy. Matter is anything that is a solid, liquid, or gas. Energy is the stuff that allows things to happen: the stuff in a battery that allows a torch to shine, the stuff in nuclear fuel that makes bombs explode, the stuff in your breakfast that keeps you going 'til lunch.

Hot on Heat

One especially important type of energy is heat. Heat is actually just molecules (see page 124) wobbling about. The more they wobble, the more heat there is. Heat moves in three ways, which are demonstrated by this pan of soup:

The soup bubbles, swirls and steams, spreading heat through **convection**.

The pan is hot because heat travels through the metal it is made of by **conduction**.

You can feel the heat from the flames without touching them, because the heat travels to you by **radiation**.

In contrast, cold is just a lack of heat. This means you can't create cold, you can only move heat somewhere else. For instance, the inside of a refrigerator is only cold because the heat is released via the coils of pipe at the back. In fact, refrigerators actually help to warm the rooms they are in.

THE LAWS OF MOTION

Physicists use particular words to describe the way things move. Here's a selection with descriptions of their meanings:

Speed: the distance something moves in a specific amount of time (it is measured in m per second).

Velocity: speed in a particular direction (m per second).

Acceleration: the rate of increase in velocity over a specific amount of time (m per second per second).

Force: the amount of "push"—the thing that is needed to make an object accelerate or change direction (newtons).

Work: when a force moves an object, "work" has been done on the object. If you lift a box, the amount of work you do is more the heavier the box is, or the higher you lift it (joules).

Power: the amount of work done in a given time (watts).

Kinetic energy: the energy an object has due to its motion (joules).

Galileo and Newton

An Italian named Galileo figured out a lot of the physics of motion 400 years ago. He developed scientific theories by doing experiments rather than just talking about how the world might work, the way the ancient Greeks did. An Englishman named Isaac Newton then improved on Galileo's theories and came up with these Laws of Motion:

1. Unless forces are applied to them, objects stay in place or keep moving in straight lines without changing velocity.

2. If a force is applied to an object, it will change velocity and direction. The bigger the force, the bigger the change.

3. If you push something, it pushes back just as hard (which is why it hurts your hand if you hit something).

The Ups and Downs of Waves

Waves are important because they are everywhere, from outer space to the center of the Earth. There is a special set of words to describe them, too:

Frequency: the number of peaks passing any point (between the two dotted lines, for example) in a second—measured in "hertz."

Wavelength: the distance between two identical points.

Peak: the highest point of a wave.

Trough: the lowest point of a wave.

Amplitude: the height of a wave from peak to trough.

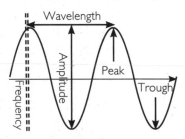

Two of the most well-known waves are light waves and sound waves. They come in handy when you want to see or hear anything, but are very different from each other. The different colors you see are light waves of different frequencies—from low-frequency red through the colors in a rainbow, to high-frequency violet. You hear sound waves of different frequencies as different pitches—the higher the frequency, the higher the note.

A wave of yellow light travels at 299,792,458 m per second in a vacuum (a completely empty space with no air in it). The length of a wave of light is just 0.00057 mm! Sound waves are very different. For instance, the note middle C on a piano measures 790 mm and travels from the piano to your ear at about 330 m per second. If you were to place the piano under water, the sound of the notes would actually travel more quickly, at about 1,500 m per second.

ELECTRICITY
AND MAGNETISM

Electrons (see page 124) are tiny particles that make up the outer layers of atoms, but they can easily be removed. When this happens, these "free" electrons cause different types of electricity. If they move, along a wire, for instance, they cause an electric current useful for making lights light up. If they stay in one place, they cause static electricity, which you might hear crackling when you take your pullover off. If you take it off in a dark room, you might even see some flashes and glows, too.

You won't be surprised to hear that magnetism is the property that magnets have. The Earth itself is a huge magnet. Every magnet has two areas called poles—a north pole and a south pole, just like the Earth. Each pole attracts (pulls) poles of the opposite type and repels (pushes away) poles of the same type. This is why the Earth's North Pole attracts the red end of a compass needle, which is the south pole of a little magnet itself.

Electricity and magnetism are closely related—if you send electricity along a wire, the wire becomes slightly magnetic. Likewise, if you wave a magnet about near a wire, a small amount of electricity is created. The area round a magnet where the effects of the magnetism can be detected is called a magnetic field. The area around a charged object is called an electric field. If you put a magnet under a piece of paper and sprinkle iron filings (powdered iron) on it, you can actually see the pattern the magnetic field makes. (You can do without the paper if you don't mind spending the rest of the day picking the iron filings off the magnet.)

SPACE, TIME, AND ALL THAT

The fact that planets spin and orbit the sun seems obvious now, but people once believed that the sun was moving around the Earth. Now we know that the reason the sun rises in the east, travels across the sky, and sets in the west is because we are watching it from a spinning planet, but it took absolutely ages for people to work this out (after all, they couldn't just nip up to outer space to have a look).

The Earth rotates, the moon orbits the Earth, and the Earth orbits the sun. These movements give us the lengths of our days, months, and years. However, on Neptune, which is much farther away from the sun, a year is about 165 times longer than a year on Earth. This is because it takes so much longer for Neptune to orbit the sun. If you lived there, you'd never have a birthday.

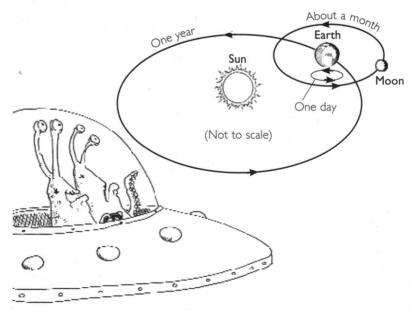

One year

About a month

Earth

Sun

Moon

One day

(Not to scale)

GRAVITY AND BLACK HOLES

Gravity is the force that causes apples to fall to the ground and the moon to move. In fact, every object in the universe pulls on every other object with the force of gravity. The closer objects are together and the more massive they are, the stronger the pull.

Gravity is usually a weak force—it is only really noticeable when at least one large object, such as the Earth, is involved. The Earth is pretty much spherical in shape—its gravitational pull draws everything toward its center, making a sphere. However, the spinning of the Earth pushes everything out a little around the equator, so it is a bit like the shape of a slightly squashed ball (called an oblate spheroid, in fact).

Sometimes, however, gravity can be a very strong force indeed. If you had superhuman strength and could crush enough stuff (anything would do) into a tiny volume, you would get so much gravitational force that even light would be sucked in—and create what is called a black hole. If you got too close to a black hole, you would be squeezed by the gravitational force and pulled into a long thin strand—very unpleasant.

Did You Know?

Albert Einstein discovered that strong gravity actually slows the flow of time. This means that if you did lurk about by a black hole for a while, you might find that a century has passed at home, while you had only lived through a year.

QUICK CHEMISTRY

Chemistry is the branch of science that looks at substances called elements and how they react together. Everything in the universe—including the Earth itself and everything on it—is made of 94 different natural elements. (Scientists have learned to make a few more, but most of those go *pffft* and disappear after less than a second.)

Atoms and Molecules

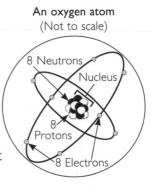

An oxygen atom
(Not to scale)

8 Neutrons
Nucleus
8 Protons
8 Electrons

Oxygen, hydrogen, water, and your body are all made of tiny particles called atoms. Atoms have a small dense area in the middle—the nucleus—which usually contains a mixture of protons (each with a positive electrical charge) and neutrons (with no electrical charge). Most of an atom is occupied by negatively charged electrons.

Often, atoms join together to make molecules. An oxygen molecule is made of two oxygen atoms. A water molecule is made of two hydrogen atoms and one oxygen atom.

In a State

All substances can be divided into solids, liquids, or gases (called states or phases). In solids the atoms or molecules are stuck together, so solids are hard to pull apart. In liquids, they can move past each other, so liquids are runny. In gases they drift away from each other, so gases expand to fill whatever container they are in. Scientists often now include plasma as the fourth state or phase of matter. This is a fluid state that occurs when atoms are heated to very high temperatures.

124

Ice, water, and water vapor are all the same substance in different phases. To change water from one phase to another, you can change its temperature. For ice (a solid) to turn into water (a liquid), it must be heated until it melts, and to turn water into water vapor (a gas), you must heat it until it boils. Usually ice melts at about 0°C and water boils at about 100°C; however, you could also change the air pressure. For instance, the higher up a mountain you go, the less pressure there is from the Earth's atmosphere (because there is less air pressing down from above), so water will boil at a lower temperature.

Metals versus Nonmetals

Most of the elements in the universe are metals, and nearly all the rest are nonmetals. Almost all metals and nonmetals can be categorized in the following ways:

Properties	Sample Metals	Sample Nonmetals
	iron, mercury, lead	oxygen, carbon, chlorine
Conducts electricity?	you bet	no chance
Conducts heat?	very well	not very well
Shiny?	usually	usually not
Try twisting a lump of it and…	…it will bend.	…it will snap.

A few elements, such as arsenic and silicon, are neither metal nor nonmetal—these are called metalloids.

Fun Facts

Here are some fascinating facts about elements:

• All living things are based on the element carbon, but the most common element in the universe is hydrogen.

• Planet Earth is made mostly of iron, and the air is made mostly of nitrogen (only 21% of the air is oxygen).

• Only mercury and bromine are liquids at room temperature and room pressure.

• It was discovered that helium existed in the sun before it was found on Earth.

• The most expensive element is californium, which costs about a million times as much as gold.

THE PERIODIC TABLE

As there are so many elements and only a few, such as gold, that can be found in a pure form, it took scientists a long time to work out what each one is. A Russian scientist named Dmitri Mendeleyev was a big help with sorting out the elements into the first periodic table, shown below:

Mendeleyev noticed that if he arranged the elements he already knew about in order of the weight of their atoms, they formed a pattern. The elements with similar properties were close together. The problem was, the table Dmitri came up with had gaps in it. He decided that there must be elements to fill the gaps, but no one had discovered them yet. Helpfully,

127

he predicted the properties of the missing elements, and sure enough, when new elements were discovered that filled the gaps, these elements had pretty much the properties he had predicted.

An Element's Properties

The periodic table contains all the key facts about each element. Here is a close-up of sodium, one element in the table:

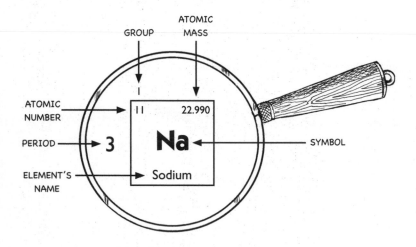

Group. Each column in the table is called a group, numbered from left to right. Elements in the same group all behave in similar ways. Elements in Group 1 are all metals that are very reactive (see opposite). For example, put sodium in water, and it rushes about going *fizzzzzzzz.*

Period. Each row on the table is called a period, numbered from top to bottom. The reactivity of elements (see opposite) changes as you move down the table. For instance, lithium is less reactive than sodium, which is less reactive than potassium, and so on.

Symbol. Each element has a symbol—often the first letter or two of its English name, but this isn't always the case. Sodium's symbol is Na because those are the first two letters of natrium, the Latin word for sodium.

Atomic number. This is the number of protons in the element's nucleus (see page 124) and its position in the periodic table.

Atomic mass. This shows the mass of the element's atom, in comparison to the mass of a hydrogen atom (which is 1.0079 atomic mass units).

Elementary Reactions

The electrons that form the outer parts of atoms occupy areas called shells. Each of these shells prefers to have a particular number of electrons in it. For instance, the first shell prefers to contain two electrons. If, as in the case of hydrogen, only one electron is present, the element will be really keen to combine with other elements—in other words, it will be very reactive.

The number of electrons in the outer shells of each element increases from left to right on the table. All the elements in group one have just one electron in their outer shells, so they are all reactive. All the elements in the last group have full shells, so they are very nonreactive.

CHEMICAL COMPOUNDS

Most natural elements are not found in a pure form. They are combined with one or more other elements to make compounds. The type of salt you might sprinkle on your food, for instance, is made from a soft metal called sodium and a poison gas called chlorine—forming what scientists call sodium chloride.

As elements often join up to make compounds, it means that there are many more compounds than elements, and lots of different ways to classify them, including:

Acids, such as citric acid (found in lemon juice) and acetic acid (found in vinegar), like to give away protons and combine with bases (see below) to make salts. Strong acids can even dissolve metal.

Bases, such as ammonia, and baking soda, and caustic soda like to take up protons (from acids, for example). Bases that dissolve in water are called alkalis.

Organic compounds, such as sugar and vitamins, contain carbon. You are made of organic compounds, too.

Minerals, such as quartz, calcite and diamond, are solids made of particular patterns of chemicals.

Rocks are mixtures of minerals and come in three types: igneous (such as granite), formed from solidified lava; sedimentary (such as limestone), formed when water containing minerals dries; and metamorphic (such as marble), formed when one type of rock changes into another.

Chemicals

Chemicals are materials made of one sort of molecule or one pattern of ions (atoms with electrons missing). They have a formula, which tells you what their molecules are made of. For instance, sulphuric acid has the formula H_2SO_4, which tells you that its molecules contain two hydrogen atoms (H), one sulphur atom (S), and four oxygen atoms (O). It can also be drawn as a diagram, shown here.

Sulphuric acid

Hydrogen And Oxygen

When you mix two elements together, they usually won't make a compound by themselves. For instance, if you were to open a big bottle of hydrogen, it would just mix with the air around it. However, if you also struck a match, the heat would cause the hydrogen from the bottle to combine with the oxygen in the air to form water.

Water is a compound of hydrogen and oxygen. Its chemical formula is H_2O—two hydrogen atoms and one oxygen atom. However, striking the match would be accompanied by a big explosion, as a result of which you would either be told off or die.

BEGINNERS BIOLOGY

Biology is the science of living things. But what exactly is a "living thing"? Fortunately, biologists have sorted out the answer: A living thing must do each of seven specific things.

Seven Signs of Life

A living thing must **(1) move**, though not necessarily from place to place—if you're a flower, opening your petals will do. It must also **(2) grow**—rather a lot if you're a blue whale, not so much if you're a germ. It must **(3) eat** or get nourishment in some way. A carrot needs sunlight and water, you might eat a carrot, a tiger might eat you—it's all nourishment. This is followed, sooner or later, by going to the bathroom (releasing waste gases if you're a carrot) or **(4) excreting**, as biologists say. A living thing must also **(5) breathe**—or take in and release gases. For instance, you take some oxygen from the air you breathe in and replace it with carbon dioxide when you breathe out, but plants take in carbon dioxide and release oxygen. **(6) Reproducing** (producing offspring) is very useful to avoid dying out. Lastly, a living thing must **(7) react**—if you scream when tickled (or grow more leaves on your sunlit side), it's one more thing that shows you're a living person (or plant).

GETTING UNDER YOUR SKIN

Throughout history many civilizations have, understandably, been a bit nervous about letting people chop up dead bodies. This meant that it took a long time to work out the basics of human anatomy—that is, what bodies look like inside and how the various bits fit together. Anatomy is only the start of understanding how the human body works, though, and even now there is still a lot that is unknown.

Body Systems

As you can see, the body is a complicated living machine. It's made up of various systems, including a digestive system (for eating), a respiratory system (for breathing), a nervous system (for control and communication), and a circulatory system (for moving your blood around).

Each system is made up of organs, which are made of tissues. All tissues are made of tiny building blocks called cells. The largest organ in the circulatory system, for

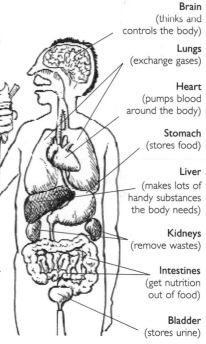

Brain
(thinks and controls the body)

Lungs
(exchange gases)

Heart
(pumps blood around the body)

Stomach
(stores food)

Liver
(makes lots of handy substances the body needs)

Kidneys
(remove wastes)

Intestines
(get nutrition out of food)

Bladder
(stores urine)

example, is the heart. It's made of a tissue called muscle. It is a blood pump, which keeps blood flowing around inside you, providing your body with the materials it needs to live and getting rid of wastes, too.

The Human Skeleton

Skull

Clavicle

Scapula

Sternum

Humerus

Vertebrae

Rib

Ulna

Radius

Pelvis

Femur

Patella

Tibia

Fibula

Your skeleton gives you your shape and allows you to move—without one, you'd be a soft, floppy heap. Your bones also help to protect you—for example, your delicate brain and eyeballs are kept safely tucked away inside a strong protective skull. Your muscles pull your bones in various directions, allowing you to walk around and lift things.

Human skeletons are built of over 200 bones, all of which contain a substance called calcium. The points where bones touch are called joints. Many of these joints are flexible—that is, they allow the bones to move. The joints in your elbows and knees are like door hinges, allowing movement in one direction only, but your thigh and shoulder joints allow movement in any direction.

The biggest bone in your body is the femur, or thigh bone, and the smallest are the ossicles, which are inside your ears. You have three in each ear—each about the size of a rice grain.

The ossicles

Hammer

Stirrup

Anvil

Did You Know?

Not all living things have skeletons, but many that do like beetles or snails—wear them on their outsides.

MICROLIFE

There are millions of trillions of trillions of living things on the Earth. Most of them are too small to see without a microscope—this is why they are called microorganisms. Most microorganisms do you no harm at all—which is just as well because they are crawling all over you right now.

However, some can make you ill or even kill you. Diseases such as tuberculosis and cholera are caused by microorganisms called bacteria, which each have only one cell. Colds and flu, however, are caused by viruses, which are halfway between living and nonliving matter, because they reproduce only by using the cells of other living things.

The Carbon Cycle

Both you and microorganisms are involved in what is called the carbon cycle. This system is all about moving carbon around, and it keeps us and our world alive. Here's how:

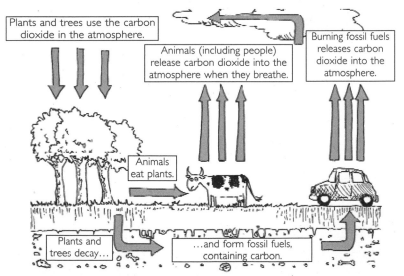

Plants and trees use the carbon dioxide in the atmosphere.

Animals (including people) release carbon dioxide into the atmosphere when they breathe.

Burning fossil fuels releases carbon dioxide into the atmosphere.

Animals eat plants.

Plants and trees decay...

...and form fossil fuels, containing carbon.

WHERE DID YOU COME FROM?

From scorching deserts to freezing mountains, there are many, many different types of habitats on Earth, but the things that live in these places are perfectly suited to their surroundings. How? A process called evolution.

Did You Know?

There's a lot of life running, flapping, and crawling about on the planet, and it all started roughly 3.7 billion years ago. Simple chemicals in the seas developed the ability to make copies of themselves. Over millions of years, these chemicals became more complex and joined with others. Eventually, tiny living things formed, each with a single cell.

Over time these creatures developed with different characteristics that helped them fit in with their habitats. So many different living things evolved that there are now over a million different "species" (types of living thing) on Earth—and scientists believe that many more are yet to be discovered.

Survival of the Fittest

Sometimes living things are born that look a little different from their parents. If this difference helps them to survive, they will be able to breed and may pass on the difference to their own children. Those animals that are stronger, faster, and able to escape predators will have the best chance of survival and reproducing.

For instance, out of a group of baby lizards born in a sandy area, those that are more sand-colored are less likely to be seen and eaten by other animals. They will survive and breed, and eventually that type of lizard will be the same color as the sand. The wings of birds are another great example of how a creature's features have changed depending on need. For example, the shape and size of some birds' wings have completely transformed over time: Penguins' wings have changed into flippers because they live near the ocean and they swim rather than fly. Vultures need to fly long distances in a steady pattern looking for food, so their wings evolved to allow them to soar. Ostriches' wings became smaller, because they don't use them at all.

INDEX

A

Africa 54, 74, 81, 86–7, 98
Alfred the Great 72
algebra 110–11
America and the Americans
    66–9, 74, 84–5
    see also United States
American Revolution 67
ancient Greece, see Greece and
    the Greeks
angles 108–11
Arabic language 47
Archimedes 114
Aristotle 52, 93
armies 54, 57, 73, 76
art and artists 30–3
Asia 54, 73, 82, 86–7
assassinations 54, 66
atomic bomb 70, 77
atoms 104, 108–9, 121, 124–29,
    131

B

biology 132–34
black holes 123

Bonaparte, Napoleon 76
books 22–27
    Adventures of Tom Sawyer, The
        24
    Anne of Green Gables 24
    Call of the Wild 23
    Jungle Book, The 26
    Little Women 27
    Old Yeller 26
    Secret Garden, The 23
    Treasure Island 27
    Wind in the Willows, The 25
    Wonderful Wizard of Oz, The 22
Britain and the British 21, 70–2,
    76–7
    see also United Kingdom

C

Caesar, Julius 54
Canute the Great 72
capital cities 80–5
carbon cycle 135
Central America 80, 84
Charles I 72, 75
chemicals 130–31
chemistry 124–131

children 22, 62, 73, 136
Churchill, Sir Winston 71
civil wars
    American 27, 67
    English 75
climate 91, 93
Cold War, the 71
Columbus, Christopher 74
composers 31
compounds 130–31
continents 80–5
countries 80–5
Crusades, The 73
Cuban Missile Crisis, The 69

D
decimal system 99–100, 115
Declaration
of Independence, The 67, 85
democracy 52, 54
dinosaurs 94–5
droughts 90

E
Earth 90–5, 110, 120–26, 135–36
earthquakes 57, 89
Einstein, Albert 70, 93, 123
electricity 121, 125
electrons 121, 124, 129, 131
elements 113, 114–17,
    116, 118–19

emperors 54
energy 118–19
England and the English 23, 30,
    72, 74
    see also Britain and the British
        and United Kingdom
English grammar 34–46
    ancient languages 47–9
    figures of speech 45–6
    homonyms
    and homophones 44
    parts of speech 36–9
    sentences 40–1
    synonyms and antonyms 44
    terminology 42–3
equator 92, 123
erosion 88
Europe and the Europeans 70,
    73–7, 83
evolution 136
explorers 74

F
Fermat, Pierre 115
Fibonacci, Leonardo 115
First World War 68, 75, 76
foreign languages 47–8
fractions 101–3
France and the French 33, 48,
    76–7
French language 48
French Revolution, The 75

G

Galileo 119
geography 78–94
geology 89, 94, 95
geometry 108–9 115
German language 48
Germany and the Germans 70,
    76–7, 83
Gettysburg Address, The 67
glaciers 88
gods and goddesses 53–7, 59–63
golden ratio 103
governments 42, 54, 67, 71, 75,
    80, 81, 84
gravity 110, 123
Greece and the Greeks 30, 52–4,
    59, 83, 104, 119
Greek alphabet 55, 102
Greek, ancient 52–9, 119

H

heat 118
Henry VIII 30, 72
history 64–77
classical history 50–63
Hitler, Adolf 70, 76–7
Holocaust, The 77
Homer 52
human body 133–34

I

Italy and the Italians 30, 32, 74,
    83, 86, 115, 119

J

Japan and the Japanese 49, 68,
    70, 77, 82
Japanese language 49
Jefferson, Thomas 66–7

K

Kennedy, John F. 66, 69
kilograms 106
kings 72–7
    Alfred the Great 72
    Canute the Great 72
    Charles I 72, 75
    Henry VIII 30–72
    Louis XVI 75
    Richard I, the Lionheart 72
    William I, the Conqueror 72

L

Labors of Heracles 62–3
Latin 55, 99, 129
laws of motion 119–20
light, speed of 120
lightning 92
Lincoln, Abraham 66–7
literature 10–27
Louis XVI, King 75

M

magnetism 121
Manhattan Project, The 70
math 96–115
measuring 96–97
Mendeleyev, Dmitri 115–16
metals and nonmetals 125
microorganisms 135
molecules 118, 124, 131
motion 119
mountains 86, 88–9
music 28–31

N

Napoleonic Wars 76
Nazis 76–7
Nero 54
Newton, Isaac 119
Nixon, Richard 66, 69
North America 73, 80, 84
numbers
   decimal system 99, 115
   Hindu–Arabic numerals 98–9,
      115
   number lines 101
   powers 105
   ratios 102
   Roman numerals 98–9
   sequences 104, 115
   square and cube 105
   triangular 104

O

Obama, Barack 66, 69
Oceania 83
oceans 87–8
Olympic Games 53
organs 133

P

periodic table 127–29
philosophy 52
physics 118–123
plasma 124
plastic 93
Plato 52
plays 12–17, 52
   Hamlet 12–13
   Macbeth 14–15
   Much Ado About Nothing 16
   Othello 15
   Romeo and Juliet 13–14
   Tempest, The 16–17
poets and poetry 18–21, 45–6,
   52
   Coleridge, Samuel Taylor 18,
      19, 21
   Dickinson, Emily 18
   Eliot, T. S. 18
   Emerson, Ralph Waldo 19
   Frost, Robert 19
   Kipling, Rudyard 19, 26
   Lear, Edward 20

Longfellow, Henry Wadsworth 20
Poe, Edgar Allen 20
Shakespeare, William 12–17, 21
Whitman, Walt 21
Wordsworth, William 21
Poles, North and South 92, 121,
powers 105
presidents 66–9
prime ministers 61–2
probability 113
pyramids, see The Seven Wonders of the Ancient World
Pythagoras 111, 114
Pythagoras's theorem 111

Q
queens 72, 58

R
ratios 102
Renaissance, The 30, 32
revolutions 67, 75
rivers 86, 87–8, 90
Richard I, the Lionheart 72
Rome and the Romans 52–63, 83, 98
Roosevelt, Franklin D. 66–8
Russia and the Russians 31, 42, 71, 73, 75–6, 82–3, 87, 127,

S
science 116–137
  biology 132–36
  chemistry 124–131
  physics 118–123
  scientists 52, 70, 90, 94. 95, 106, 108, 124, 127
seas 87
seasons 91–2
Second World War 68, 70–1, 76–7
Seven Wonders of the Ancient World 57–8
Shakespeare, William 12–17, 21
shapes 108
skeleton 134
slavery 67–8, 73
Socrates 52
Soviets 70–1, 75
South America 47, 80, 84
space 122–23
Spanish language 47
speed 110, 119
states (U.S.) 85
Station X 70
statistics 112
sun 90–2, 105, 122, 126

T
time 122
tornadoes 92
triangles 104, 108–9, 111

U

United Kingdom 83
   see also Britain and the British
United States 66–9, 71, 77, 84,
   85–7
universe 114, 118, 123–25
   see also America and
     Americans

V

Victoria, Queen 72
Vikings 74
volcanoes 86, 89

W

wars 27, 67–9, 70–1, 73, 75–7
Washington, George 66–7
water 88, 90

water cycle 90
Watergate 69
waves 120
weather 83–4
William I, the Conqueror 55, 56
Wilson, Woodrow 65, 67
World War One,
   see First World War
World War Two,
   see Second World War

Reader's Digest Books for Young Readers

Liar! Liar! Pants on Fire!

Sometimes the truth can be so strange that it's hard to believe. With hundreds of incredible true—and false—questions, kids have a great time testing their knowledge, learning fascinating truths, and uncovering lousy lies!

JAN PAYNE • 978-1-60652-476-3

i before e (except after c)
The Young Readers Edition

Full of hundreds of fascinating tidbits presented in a fun and accessible way, this lighthearted book offers kids many helpful mnemonics that make learning easy and fun.

SUSAN RANDOL • 978-1-60652-348-3

Write (Or Is That "Right"?) Every Time

Divided into bite-size chunks that include Goodness Gracious Grammar, Spelling Made Simple, and Punctuation Perfection, this book provides quick-and-easy tips and tricks to overcome every grammar challenge.

LOTTIE STRIDE • 978-1-60652-341-4

I Wish I Knew That: U.S. Presidents

Starting with who is qualified to be president, what a president does, and how the president works with the rest of the government, this book, written just for kids, quickly turns to the fascinating profiles of each of the 43 presidents. There are also sidebars filled with fun and unusual information about our leaders.

PATRICIA A. HALBERT • 978-1-60652-360-5

Other Titles Available in This Series

I Wish I Knew That: Geography
I Wish I Knew That: Math
I Wish I Knew That: Science

Teacher's guides are available at RDTradePublishing.com
Each book is $9.99 hardcover
E-book editions also available

Reader's Digest books can be purchased through retail and online bookstores. In the United States books are distributed by Penguin Group (USA), Inc. For more information or to order books, call 1-800-788-6262.